THE ROCK AND THE RABBI

THE ROCK AND THE RABBI

Life Lessons from Peter's Journey with Jesus

Andrew Sabaratnam

The Rock And The Rabbi

© 2023 by Andrew Sabaratnam

All rights reserved.

This book or any portion thereof may not be reproduced or used in any manner whatsoever without the express written permission of the publisher except for the use of brief quotations in a book review or scholarly journal.

Scripture quotations are from the ESV® Bible (The Holy Bible, English Standard Version®), copyright © 2001 by Crossway Bibles, a publishing ministry of Good News Publishers. Used by permission. All rights reserved.

Scripture quotations marked (NIV) are taken from the Holy Bible, New International Version®, NIV®. Copyright © 1973, 1978, 1984, 2011 by Biblica, Inc.™ Used by permission of Zondervan. All rights reserved worldwide.

A WORD FROM THE AUTHOR

THIS BOOK EXAMINES the spiritual transformation of Peter the rock through his relationship with his rabbi, Jesus Christ. Peter seemed to have natural leadership qualities and became the *de facto* spokesman for the Twelve (Mt 15:15; 18:21; 19:27; Mk 11:21; Lk 8:45; 12:41; Jn 6:68; 13:6-9, 36). Because Peter was such a dominant figure in the gospels, we can track his spiritual development as a believer from beginning to end. A devoted disciple of Jesus, he was outspoken and passionate. Peter was also impulsive, self-confident, impetuous, stubborn, strong-willed, and aggressive. Yet, despite his shortcomings, the Lord chose Peter not for who he was but for the person the Lord wanted Peter to be.

Peter, which means "rock", a name given to him by Jesus, started like a fragile stone. Nevertheless, Peter's intimate relationship with Jesus transformed him from a fragile stone into a mighty rock. He became a leader of a movement that challenged and defied the Roman authorities. He was the one who preached at Pentecost

(Acts 2:14-42), the one who opened the way for salvation to the Gentile world (Mt 16:16-19; Acts 8 & 10), and the preeminent spokesman for the Gentiles at the Council of Jerusalem (Acts 15:7-11). We can read the Bible to get knowledge about God. But only an intimate relationship with God will spiritually transform us, just as it did for Peter.

We will trail Peter in the four gospels and focus on key moments in his relationship with Jesus that led to Peter's transformation. Through Peter's journey with Jesus, you will also grow in the knowledge and understanding of our Lord Jesus Christ.

This book assumes that the reader has read all four gospels in the Bible and is familiar with the accounts and parables. All Bible verses are from the English Standard Version unless otherwise stated. UK English is used in this book. Hence you may find some differences in spelling and usage of words, especially if you use US English. All quotations are left in their original form.

Peter's story is our story. As our Lord loved Peter, He loves you, imperfect as you are. As our Lord transformed Peter, He transforms you through life lessons, trials, and divinely orchestrated plans. As you read this book, may you reflect on how God is refining you and equipping you to follow Him and walk in His steps. If you are struggling to live up to God's standards and expectations, you will find this book a source of comfort and hope.

If God can use a bumbling, brash fisherman called Peter, He can use you too.

As this book is a compilation of Peter's interactions with Jesus, it is also an excellent resource for pastors. There is a reflection component at the end of every chapter and is useful for group study.

Andrew Sabaratnam

ACKNOWLEDGEMENTS

MY GRATEFUL THANKS to my Lord Jesus Christ, who never ceases to amaze me. He gives me strength and determination to carry on despite interruptions and hindrances. For this, I labour and strive because I fix my hope on Him.

My gratitude also to the lecturers at Biblical Graduate School of Theology, Singapore, who taught me how to go deeper into God's word in order to experience it the way God intended.

Contents

A Word From The Author v

Acknowledgements viii

Simon the Galilean 1

The Rock Meets the Rabbi 7

Fisher of Men 14

Famous in Capernaum 23

Walking on Water 27

Religious Hypocrisy 33

Stumbling Block 37

Law, Prophets and the Messiah 45

Hook and Line for a Shekel 50

Sell Your Possessions 55

Wash Your Feet 60

Bitter Tears 68

Breakfast with Jesus 73

Be Sober-Minded 77

No Shortcuts 83

Epilogue 91

About The Author 93

Endnotes 95

-1-

SIMON THE GALILEAN

PETER'S BIRTH NAME was Simon (Mark 1:16), or Simeon (Acts 15:14). Jesus called him Peter (Greek) or Cephas (Aramaic), which means "rock", in recognition of the fact that Peter was the first apostle to acknowledge or confess Jesus as the Messiah (or Christ) and the Son of God (Jn 1:42; Mt 16:13-19). He is also referred to or identified as *Simon Bar-Jonah* (meaning Simon, the son of Jonah) (Mt 16:17), and as Simon Peter (Mt 16:16), combining his birth name with the name given to him by Jesus.

Some seven hundred years before Christ, Galilee's Israelite inhabitants were conquered by Assyria and were relocated to Assyria while non-Jewish immigrants moved into Galilee (2 Kgs 15:29-17:24). This is why the Bible sometimes refers to the area as "Galilee of the Gentiles" (Isa 9:1; Mt 4:13-16).

Peter was the son of Jonah[1] (Mt 16:17). Peter came from Bethsaida (Jn 1:44), a Jewish city with Greek influence, believed to be located on the northern shore of the Sea of Galilee. In this book, Peter will also be referred to as Simon or Simon Peter. These names will be used interchangeably.

Peter, being a Galilean, spoke in a northern Aramaic dialect[2], and with a distinct accent that was not easy to hide (Mt 26:69; 73). Galileans naturally stood out to the people of Jerusalem. Judeans tended to look down on Galileans because of their lack of Jewish sophistication, compounded by their greater openness to Hellenistic influence[3] (Jn 1:46; 7:52). Yet it was all part of God's plan that Jesus was to grow up in Galilee (Mt 2:19–23). Being Galilean, Jesus was despised and was held in low esteem (Isa 53:3). The fact that Jesus lived and ministered in Galilee is yet another example of His identification with those the world rejects. In Galilee, Jesus recruited most of His disciples, including Peter (Mt 4:17-23), started His ministry, and performed His first miracle (Jn 2:11).

Peter moved to Capernaum (Mk 1:21; 29-30) and settled there for unknown reasons. Capernaum (the village of Nahum, which may have been the traditional hometown of the Old Testament prophet) was also the home of Andrew, James, John, and Matthew, the tax collector (Mt 9:9). Jesus taught in the synagogue and did many miracles here. Jesus healed the Centurion's servant (Lk 7:1-10), two blind men (Mt 9:27-31), Peter's mother-in-law, the paralysed man who was lowered through the roof (Mk 2:1-12), a man with a withered hand (Mt 12:9-13), a woman with issue of blood (Mk 5:25-34), and a man who was possessed (Mt 9:32-34). He also brought Jairus' daughter back from the dead (Lk 8:40-56).

Peter was a fisherman (Mk 1:16). He and his brother Andrew were in partnership with John and James, the two sons of Zebedee (Lk 5:10). It is highly probable that Peter remained a fisherman even when he was a disciple of Jesus (Jn 21:3).

The Bible does not specifically give the ages of any of the original twelve disciples. To determine Peter's age, let us first examine the Jewish education system of the first century. At age five, young boys went to the local synagogue school to learn Hebrew and memorise the Torah. By the time of his *bar mitzvah*[4] at age thirteen, a typical Jewish young man was very conversant with God's Word, having memorised the *Torah* (Pentateuch), the *Neviim* (The Prophets), and the *Kituvin* (The Writings), which comprised all of the *Tanakh* (Hebrew Bible) of that day.[5]

After that, they went on to learn a trade as an apprentice. Marriage was encouraged by about age eighteen to twenty. For those who wanted to become a disciple to a rabbi, they attended the *bet midrash* (house of study), at about age fifteen. While adults could join in the sessions with the Rabbi, the disciples (or students) were generally younger than their teacher.[6]

Scripture teaches that Jesus was about thirty years old when He began His public ministry (Lk 3:23). He was recognised as a rabbi by a broad section of the people: private individuals (Lk12:13), lawyers (Lk.10:25), the rich young ruler (Lk 18:18), the Pharisees (Lk 19:39), and the Sadducees (Lk 20:27). It is likely that the disciples of Jesus were under thirty years of age. Jesus also referred to them as "little children" (Jn 13:33), possibly indicating that they were several years younger.

As mentioned earlier, Peter worked as fishermen. This means that he was old enough to work full time. Peter, together with Andrew and James and John, probably worked on small wooden boats no more than 6 metres (18 feet to 20 feet) long. They used nets made of linen. These nets were visible during the day and so they fished at night. The nets had to be washed and dried at the end of each day or they would rot. Each boat had four men to man the boat and handle the nets.[7]

Peter was already married (1 Cor 9:5) when he began following Jesus. His sick mother-in-law is mentioned in Matthew 8:14. This means Peter was at least 18 years of age. However, only Peter and Jesus seem to be concerned about the temple tax (Mt 17:24-27) which was required only by men over twenty.[8] None of the other eleven was mentioned. So, Peter was significantly older than the other apostles, perhaps already in his mid-twenties, when Jesus' ministry began.

Anyone who heard Peter's Galilean accent, would assume him to be an unschooled ordinary man (Acts 4:13). Historical facts seem to be lacking to make a reasonable conclusion whether Peter was poor or not, and how well educated he was. But his economic situation was far from unfavourable. Geographical reports[9] indicate that there were successful fish-pickling centres surrounding the Sea of Galilee. For example, the city of Magadan (Mt 15:39), more commonly known as Magdala (Aramaic) or Migdal (Hebrew), where Mary Magdalene was from, was also named "place of salted fish" in Greek (*Taricheae*). Several historical sources, such as Flavius Josephus, Cicero, Suetonius, and Strabo, claim that Magdala became self-sufficient as a result of the export of salted fish.[10] Fish exports were in considerable demand not only to the inhabitants in the region, but also the fish-shops in Jerusalem, the Roman army, and the commerce of the Roman empire outside of Israel.[11] The name *Tarichos* ("salted fish") became the city's international "brand," since pickled fish was sold to Rome.[12] It is a great wonder, then, that the future disciples in Galilee took Jesus' invitation to leave everything and follow Him.

When Jesus, the God incarnate, lived and walked among us, Israel was under Rome's rule. There were frequent uprisings and riots. Also, several influential parties emerged in Israel. The Pharisees were religious conservatives who were known for their piety. The Sadducees were more liberal and cooperated with Rome. Furthermore, they denied the resurrection. The Zealots opposed all cooperation with Rome, and were terrorists. Israel's religious community was looking forward to the Messiah's coming with anticipation. Peter, a fisherman, met Jesus during this time, became His disciple, shadowed

Him for three years, witnessed His crucifixion and resurrection, and became a transformed leader whose first sermon led five thousand people (Acts 4:4) to Christ.

Reflection

Before Peter met Jesus, he was a fisherman who was not very educated and spoke only Aramaic. Peter was originally from Bethsaida and later relocated to Capernaum, perhaps for job opportunities. Some years later, on the shores of Galilee, he met Jesus Christ, who radically changed his life. However, this did not happen overnight. Peter underwent three years of training, under the tutelage of Jesus.

Take a moment to reflect on your life, from birth until now. Consider the people you met along the way. Nothing happens by accident. God has planned your life. Before God shaped you in the womb, He knew all about you. Before you saw the light of day, He had holy plans for you (cf. Jer 1:5a). Think about how you came to accept Christ. You did not choose Jesus; He chose you and appointed you so that you might go and bear fruit for God (cf. Jn 15:16). A clear understanding of your purpose will help you live intentionally and passionately daily.

What are your strengths?

What are God's gifts and talents for you?

What is God's purpose for your life?

–2–
THE ROCK MEETS THE RABBI
(JN 1:35-42)

ROMAN OPPRESSION MADE the Jews of Jesus' day long for the Messiah. So, when John the Baptiser came with the message that the Messiah's coming was imminent, many responded to John's message to repent so that they would be prepared to meet the Messiah (Mk 1:4-5). Whether out of curiosity, political interest, or some other motive, Andrew and John (the brother of James) became John's disciples (Jn 1:40)[13], and spent time listening to a poor, rugged, holy man giving speeches.

Our story begins at Bethany (not to be confused with Bethany near Jerusalem) in the Jordan valley, north of the Dead Sea, where John was baptising (Jn 1:28). Now, Jesus went from Galilee to the Jordan River to be baptised by John (Mt 3:13; Mk 1:9-11; Lk 3:21-22). John knew Jesus since Jesus was a relative, but until the event of the baptism, John did not know that Jesus was the Messiah. Although they lived miles apart, John may have heard reports about Jesus and considered Him holy (Mt 3:13-15). But John still did not know who the Messiah was.

John must have asked God to reveal the Messiah to Him in a unique way, and God granted John a sign. John 1:33 implies this. The sign was the Holy Spirit descending upon the Messiah. When the sign occurred, and the Holy Spirit descended upon Jesus during His baptism, John knew Jesus was the Messiah. Now he was able to proclaim that Jesus is the Messiah.

Why did Jesus need to get baptised? Neither Mark nor Luke addresses the question (Mk 1:9–11; Lk 3:21–22). John doesn't describe Jesus' baptism in detail but emphasises His anointing as the Son of God as the Spirit descended on Him through baptism (Jn 1:32–34). Matthew is the only gospel writer to raise this issue, as he includes a piece of the story that the other gospel writers do not, that John himself was hesitant to baptise Jesus. John, aware that Jesus wasn't just another person coming to repent and confess his sins, protests: *"I need to be baptized by you, and do you come to me?"* (Mt 3:14).

But Jesus answered him, "Let it be so now, for thus it is fitting for us to fulfill all righteousness" (Mt 3:15). Jesus saw His life as the fulfilment of all righteousness. He who was without sin submitted to a baptism for sinners. As a result of this act, the Saviour of the world took His place among sinners. He wanted to fulfill the righteousness required not of Himself but of every sinful man.

Immediately after His baptism, Jesus was led by the Holy Spirit into the desert to be tempted by the devil for forty days and nights (Mt 4:1-11; Mk 1:12-13; Lk 4:1-13). Why? The reason is provided in Hebrews 2:17: *Therefore he had to be made like his brothers in every respect, so that he might become a merciful and faithful high priest in the service of God, to make propitiation for the sins of the people.*

After His return from the desert, Jesus is spotted by John the Baptiser. John tells his two disciples, Andrew, and John (the brother of James) (Jn 1:29), *"Behold, the Lamb of God!"* The disciples then left John's side and set out after Jesus. John the Baptiser had said, *"He must increase, but I must decrease"* (Jn 3:30). John helped his disciples understand the significance of Jesus, making it easy for them to leave his side and follow the Saviour.

As Andrew and John begin to draw near to Jesus, He turns around, and seeing that they were following Him, initiates the conversation and asks, *"What do you seek?"* (Jn 1:38a) Jesus does not ask them, *"Whom do you seek?"* but *"What do you seek?"*. Jesus wanted these disciples to evaluate what exactly it was that they were seeking from Him. (Compare this with John 6:26 where the reason a crowd was following Jesus was to be fed.)

"Rabbi, where are You staying?" (Jn 1:38b). Their reply could be taken as either they were caught off guard by the question or were actually asking Jesus in a polite way to be His disciples. Our Lord's answer is encouraging: *"Come and see"* (Jn 1:39). In Luke 9:57-58, someone said to Jesus that

he would follow Him wherever He goes. *And Jesus said to him, "Foxes have holes and birds of the air have nests, but the Son of Man has nowhere to lay his head"* (Lk 9:58). So, Jesus does not just invite anybody to follow Him.

Let us briefly examine first-century discipleship. Rabbis ran schools and would carefully select their students. A rabbi only selected those who he thought could fully measure up to his standard and eventually become just like him. Jesus alluded to this in Luke 6:40 when He said that a fully trained student will be like his teacher. As the rabbi lived and taught his understanding of scripture, his students listened and watched and imitated so as to become like him. If a student wanted to study with a rabbi, he would ask if he might "follow" the rabbi. Some were invited to "follow" the rabbi. When a rabbi says, "follow me", he meant, "come and be with me as my disciple and submit to my authoritative teaching."[14] This indicated that the rabbi believed that the potential disciple had the ability and commitment to become like him.[15] Those who were not qualified enough to become disciples, would instead choose a vocation, like farming, fishing, carpentry, or the like. (This explains why the religious leaders looked down on the disciples of Jesus.)[16] By becoming a rabbi's disciple, the young student readily agrees to totally surrender to the rabbi's authority in all areas of interpreting the Scriptures for his life.

When Jesus encouraged John's two disciples to come and see where He was staying, He seemed to be inviting them to follow Him as His disciples. Andrew and John (the brother of James) spent the day with Jesus. After their time with Jesus, Andrew and John left convinced that John the Baptiser was right.

Andrew went back to Peter and exclaimed, *"We have found the Messiah!"* Andrew brought Peter to Jesus. Andrew is mentioned only a few times in the New Testament, but on each occasion, we see him introducing others (Jn 6:8-9; Jn.12:20-22) to the Lord Jesus. Here, he had the supreme joy of introducing his brother Peter to the Lord (Jn 1:39-42).

Jesus looked at him and said, "You are Simon the son of John. You shall be called Cephas" (which means Peter) (Jn 1:42).[17] (Cephas is Aramaic for *"rock"* and Peter is the Greek version.) The word 'look' is intended to give the impression that Peter experienced the intent gaze of Jesus. But Jesus' gaze was not focused on the externals of this fisherman. He looked into and saw the heart of who Simon was and what he would become *and needed no one to bear witness about man, for he himself knew what was in man* (Jn 2:25).

It is not uncommon for rabbis to rename their disciples.[18] However this change of name happens only for Peter and no other disciple. Peter's name change, which comes from Jesus Himself, is intended to indicate a special function. The renaming of Simon as the "rock" did not immediately transform Peter into the person Jesus wanted him to be. Jesus needed time to work on Him. One of the primary purposes for Jesus in His relationship with Peter was to accomplish this training so that Peter becomes the "rock".[19]

In John 15:16a, Jesus tells His disciples, *"You did not choose me, but I chose you and appointed you."* Peter, on his own free will, went to meet Jesus. Yet Jesus was expecting Peter and had divinely chosen him. We see a similar incident in John 1:43-51, where Nathanael goes on his own free will with Philip to meet Jesus only to find out that Jesus was expecting him and knew all about him. These are examples of the harmony between the free will of man and the sovereign will of God.

Andrew and John were overjoyed to have a chance meeting with Jesus, but little did they know how special they were in God's great redemption plan. When Peter met Jesus, it was out of curiosity, but little did he know the pivotal role he would play in God's great plan, and that Jesus would hand him *the keys to the kingdom of heaven* (Mt 16:19).

Was it mere coincidence that Andrew and John happened to be with John the Baptiser when Jesus walked by? The Bible tells us that we can make our plans, but it is God who directs our steps (Pr 16:9). It is beyond our understanding that no matter how small and tiny we are compared to His greatness and vastness, He knows our going and coming, our thoughts, our words, the meditations of our hearts, the tears we shed, and the number of hairs on our heads! We are significant to God.

We don't always have the big picture to show us what God is doing and why He is doing it but we know He is in control. All our circumstances, events, and meetings are really the outworking of God's plans. *And we know that for those who love God all things work together for good, for those who are called according to his purpose* (Rm 8:28).

God allows all circumstances in our lives, and uses them to build godly character, to teach us to exercise our faith, and to redirect our lives. Some circumstances may take us out of our comfort zones. When life deals us circumstances that we don't understand we can choose to become better or bitter. If we focus on the trials, we can become bitter. If we open up to God to speak to us through our circumstances, we become better. For this reason, we must *give thanks in all circumstances; for this is God's will for you in Christ Jesus* (1 Thes 5:18).

Reflection

God will use everyday circumstances and conditions to grab our attention, to prompt us to hear His voice, to direct our path, or to answer a prayer. Have you ever been in a difficult situation that turned out to be a blessing in disguise?

Can you recall instances when a 'chance' meeting with someone resulted in an answer to prayer?

Has God ever used uncomfortable circumstances to prevent you from drifting away and to draw you back to Him?

Consider all the circumstances God has used to shape you. How has God used circumstances to shape your faith to trust Him?

-3-
Fisher of Men
(Luke 5:1-11)

THE OFFICIAL CALL to Peter by Jesus to be fisher of men is covered Mark 1:16-17, Matthew 4:18-19 and Luke 5:1-11, and their versions vary a lot between gospels. Matthew's version emphasises Jesus' regal authority. In Luke's version, Peter, James, and John (Andrew is not mentioned) are overwhelmed by Jesus' fish miracle and leave everything to follow the master. Luke also places the story of Peter's mother-in-law before the call story, while Mark does it after the call to be fishers of men. Taken at face value, the gospels seem to provide sequential account of Christ's life: from birth, baptism, temptation, ministry, passion, death and then resurrection. However, a closer comparison of the order of their accounts reveals several points at which they differ over the sequence of events. The accounts are historically accurate and, in their general outline, chronologically accurate, but the events and teaching of Jesus' life are not necessarily arranged chronologically but along topical or thematic lines.

"If the gospels contradict each other, they only do so in the minor, secondary, peripheral details. They're completely harmonious in the core details of the story. Dr William Lane Craig [apologist and philosopher] said "Historians expect to find inconsistencies like these even in the most reliable sources. No historian simply throws out a source because it has inconsistencies". Historians look at whether accounts harmonise in the primary details. If they conflict only in the peripherals, they don't throw the sources out."[20]

In John 1:35-42, Peter, Andrew and John met Jesus and trusted Him. This was covered in Chapter 2. They probably followed Him at times, but they also carried on with their fishing business. Let us now examine the call story as told by Luke as more details are given in the passage. Luke 4:37 says: *And reports about him went out into every place in the surrounding region.* Jesus was already famous for His miracles and Peter, Andrew, James and John must have witnessed them.

In Luke 5:1-11, Simon and company had just finished fishing. They had spent a long and fruitless night fishing. Chapter 1 explains why they fished at night. Simon and Andrew were probably cleaning up their fishing equipment, and nearby, John and James were probably mending their nets. Suddenly, a crowd began to gather near their boats. Simon looked up and there was Jesus. The people had found Him walking along the beach and pressed Him to talk to them. They wanted to hear *the word of God* (Lk 5:1). Jesus agreed. He got into Simon's boat to be better heard. You would think that Simon

Peter and Andrew, James and John, who were disciples of Jesus, would be beside Him, close to the Master. Instead, the crowds pressed upon Jesus, and the disciples were at a distance, tending to business, washing their nets. They seemed detached from the Master and from the crowd.

When Jesus had finished speaking, He may have wanted to do something good for Peter for using his boat. Jesus commands Peter, "*Put out into the deep and let down your nets for a catch*" (Lk 5:4b). Earlier on (Lk 5:3) Jesus had disrupted his work when He sat in one of the boats and asked Peter to put the boat a little from shore. Now He wants Peter to go fishing again. Simon Peter replied rather irritatingly, "*Master, we worked hard all night and caught nothing, but at Your bidding I will let down the nets*" (Lk 5:5).

Now let's think about this. Peter had years of experience with fishing, and he knew that if he did not catch anything during the night, the chances of a good catch during the day would be even smaller. Moreover, the nets would be visible in the daytime (see Chapter 1 for details). Peter was dead tired after a night of fruitless work. Perhaps Peter thought of Jesus as a rabbi who spoke with authority, and who had the power to do miracles, but what did He know about catching fish? Peter is really no different from many of us. Oftentimes we think we have better judgement than God. We actually believe that what we want and how we want it is better than the way God can bring it to us.

Even though it contradicted his professional experience, Peter and the others obediently did as Jesus instructed. The catch was so huge that the nets began to break, and two boats were needed to fill the catch, almost to the brink of the boats sinking. There was an unprecedented catch of fish in an area that appeared hopelessly unproductive the night before. All of this occurred due to the powerful and authoritative words of Jesus. This was probably the most successful catch of their careers. Imagine the handsome profit they would make at the local market with two boatloads of fish! If Jesus could be a partner in their fish business, they would be very rich soon!

But that was not what was in Peter's mind. Peter had already been in contact with Jesus a great deal. He had seen Him do miracles, including the healing of many and the casting out of evil spirits. But this miracle, was directed to him and the other disciples and to his personal trade. It hit home for Peter. Who is this man who can command the fish and tell the fishermen the exact spot to find them? Peter thought he was the expert, but now he sees that Jesus is Lord of the sea as well. The miracle of the fish made Peter feel a sense of inferiority and also see something of his own heart. Peter fell on his knees before Jesus and said, *"Depart from me, for I am a sinful man, O Lord"* (Lk 5:8). Jesus was no longer just His Master. Peter now saw Jesus as *"Lord"*, the One who controls all the circumstances of life.

Peter recognises his unworthiness, and he confesses his sinfulness to Jesus. He was the only disciple recorded in all the gospels to do so. When the prophets or apostles of Scripture had a direct encounter with God for the first time, there was an immediate awareness of their unworthiness. Moses hid his face (Ex 3:6), Isaiah cried and confessed his sins (Is 6:5), and John fell at his feet as though dead (Rev 1:17). A person can't go very far with God until he or she discovers his or her own sinfulness and the corruptness of his or her heart.

What followed after Peter's confession was an invitation by Jesus to leave everything and follow Him. Jesus tells him, *"Do not be afraid; from now on you will be catching men"* (Lk 5:10b). Usually, the training from a rabbi was to enable the disciple to become a teacher of the Law. In this case, Jesus calls Peter, not to be a teacher of the Law, but to be a fisher of men.

What lessons can we learn from this episode? Jesus could have commanded the fish to just jump into the boats, but He instructed Peter to fish. Peter was being trained to trust and obey Jesus. Peter's recognition of his own sinfulness did not disqualify him from serving the Lord. The Lord calls into His service those who are constantly, painfully aware of their own sinfulness and weakness, because they are the only ones who are also constantly aware of their need to rely totally on Him. If you know the depravity of your own heart, you will deeply appreciate the abundant grace that the Lord offers.

When Jesus gave the initial call to Peter and the others (Jn 1:35-42), they did not leave their trade. In Luke 5, when Jesus called them again, *they pulled their boats up on shore, left everything and followed him* (Lk 5:11). This time they truly left everything. They were not going to fish for a while. This is confirmed in Matthew 19:27a where Peter tells Jesus, *"See, we have left everything and followed you."* Other than in Matthew 17:27 (where Jesus instructs Peter to cast a hook to retrieve a shekel from the mouth of the first fish he catches, to pay for Jesus' tax and Peter's), the next time we see all of them return to their trade is in John 21:3, after the resurrection of Jesus and before Jesus meets the disciples at the beach and restores Peter.

While they fully committed their time to Jesus, the fishing was probably done by hired labourers because Mark 1:20 mentions that the sons of Zebedee had hired servants in the boat. Zebedee and his sons owned a sizeable business, and Andrew and Peter were partners. Zebedee owned his boats and hired day labourers.[21]

As mentioned earlier, after Peter was first introduced by Andrew to Jesus (Jn 1:42), Peter would probably have accompanied Jesus during His early Judean ministry (John 1:42-4:43) and witnessed first-hand all the miracles Jesus did. Then he resumed his occupation as a fisherman. According to scholars, a year had passed between Peter's first meeting and the call to be a fisher of men. We are not told if Peter was fishing on a full-time or part-time basis. But it is obvious, between the first meeting and the calling, that Peter was not fully committed to Jesus. Jesus was not able to use Peter effectively if Peter was not fully committed to Jesus.

Becoming a born-again Christian is the same. It must involve a serious and genuine commitment to become a devoted disciple or follower of Jesus Christ, in every part of our lives. We cannot be just a fan or spectator. When we make that decision to follow Jesus, we need to do so in the way that He meant us to. Jesus wants us to do far more than simply agree with Him or even believe in Him. He also wants us to hand our entire lives over to Him and to follow Him with total commitment.

Perhaps Peter had fears about giving up his job totally. Perhaps he was not fully convinced about Jesus being the Messiah. Rabbi yes, but Messiah...not sure. Jesus knew the inner struggle Peter had and instead of berating him or coercing him to be fully committed, the Lord waited patiently, until Peter was ready to commit fully.

Jesus had done many miracles and people had marveled at His power and teaching, but no one had concluded, as Peter did, that Jesus was so righteous, and that he was so wretched. Something happened that made Peter see Jesus in a new light and at the same moment, was overwhelmed with his own sinfulness. Peter must have seen Jesus do many miracles, but they all lay outside his experience and were just mysteries to him. It was different with fish; he knew everything about fish. Unlike the other miracles, he was struck by this miracle.

Seeing the glory of the Lord in light of his own sinfulness filled Peter with fear. And here we see Jesus reaching out to Peter with the words, *"Do not be afraid"* and with the charge, *"from now on you will be catching men"* (Lk 5:10).

There was considerable time between the first meeting and Peter's commitment to God. Didn't Jesus have big plans for Peter? After all He had given him a new name to fit the task Jesus had for him. Yet Jesus was not in a hurry. What was important was for Peter to repent and allow Jesus to have complete control of his life. Perhaps recollecting this event led Peter to say in 2 Peter 3:9 - *The Lord is not slow to fulfill his promise as some count slowness, but is patient toward you, not wishing that any should perish, but that all should reach repentance.*

Reflection

How long have you been a Christian? What made you become a Christian? What made you decide that you needed a Saviour? How would you describe your relationship with Lord?

If God called you today to carry out a divine task, would you do it joyfully or would you procrastinate? God's calling will undoubtedly require you to step outside your comfort zone. After all, Jesus never hesitated to tell people to leave their everyday lives and follow Him on an unfamiliar path.

If you are currently serving the Lord in church or elsewhere, are you doing it because you truly love your Saviour and will go out of your comfort zone to please Him, or are you doing it out of obligation, routine, or because it seems to be the right thing to do? If we truly loved Jesus, we would do anything for Him, no matter the cost. This kind of sacrificial love never goes unnoticed and will always be rewarded! Jesus said so Himself (Mt 19:29).

Would Jesus say to you, *"Well done, good and faithful servant,"* if you entered heaven today?

- 4 -
FAMOUS IN CAPERNAUM
(MARK 1:35-39)

NOW JESUS WAS in Capernaum and healed many who were sick with various diseases and cast out an evil spirit. The following account is recorded in Mark 1:21-39. It was the Sabbath day. After preaching in the synagogue, Jesus was confronted by a demon-possessed man. Jesus cast out that evil spirit. He left the synagogue and went to Peter's house, presumably for lunch (Mk 1:31). When He arrived, Jesus found Peter's mother-in-law sick with a fever. Jesus healed her. When sundown came and the Sabbath was over, all the people in Capernaum brought their sick and those possessed with demons for Jesus to heal them. He does this, no doubt meeting people and helping them way into the night. It must have been a demanding day (and night) for Jesus. Simon Peter goes from fishing to hosting the most famous person in Capernaum. Simon Peter's home became a popular destination for healing.

The next day, very early in the morning, while it was still dark, Jesus went to a desolate place to pray. Jesus wanted uninterrupted and unhindered prayer time. His prayer time was precious and private, and He wanted nothing to come between Him and time spent in His Father's presence.

Meanwhile at Peter's home, the crowd presumably returned, asking for Jesus and disrupted Peter's household. Peter may have gone looking for Jesus but found that the Lord was not there. And so, he may have initiated a search, probably along with James and John and his brother Andrew, to find where Jesus was, and when they found Him, they interrupted Jesus and said, *"Everyone is looking for you"* (Mk 1:37). Peter probably thought that Jesus would be pleased to know that everyone was looking for Him. The disciples did not understand that Jesus did not desire this popular acclaim. Also, popularity and power were a distant echo to Jesus' wilderness temptation (cf. Lk 4:7-8).

Jesus probably prayed to overcome the temptation to take the popular route. Jesus also probably sought God's direction for the day. When Peter came looking for Him, Jesus said confidently, *"Let us go on to the next towns, that I may preach there also, for that is why I came out"* (Mk 1:38). Jesus corrects Peter gently, teaching Peter about the need for His ministry to spread more widely. Peter observed how Jesus did not let anything influence His sound judgement. Peter saw how Jesus spent much time in prayer. In years to come Peter would pen down these words, *"The end of all things is at hand; therefore be self-controlled and sober-minded for the sake of your prayers"* (1 Peter 4:7).

If Jesus, God in human flesh, felt the need for prayer in His life, then all the more do we need to make prayer a priority in our own lives. There are times when we think what we do is the right thing because it seems noble, and for God's glory. We embark on it and pray to God to bless our efforts. Then it backfires, and we wonder why. Perhaps we should have waited patiently upon the Lord and sought His wisdom and direction first rather and then make assumptions for God. Prayer helps us overcome temptation, determine God's will, and accomplish His work.

Reflection
Our lives are filled with busy schedules, draining jobs, endless bills, interrupting phone messages, and demanding relationships. It's a fact of modern life. Our busy lives make it challenging to spend quiet time with God. We race through a short passage of Scripture and our prayer requests, while keeping an eye on the phone to ensure that we get all the important text. Does this sound like you?

Are you concerned that setting aside time for Bible study and prayer will take up valuable time that could be used for other activities? Or do you spend a few minutes reading a devotional and praying quickly so that you won't feel guilty? Shouldn't you be able to schedule unhurried time with God if you can schedule other things? If it was important to Jesus, how much more is it to you? He even walked away from the needy crowds to pray.

When you are still before God, you build your relationship with Him, experience His peace, and draw strength from Him to face the day ahead. There will probably never be a time when you are less busy. But how can less time with God be a solution? If you have been neglecting your quiet time with God, you may need to make significant changes in your life.

How do you schedule your quiet time with God? When do you meet with Him? Do you look forward to your quiet time?

-5-

WALKING ON WATER
(MATTHEW 14:22-33)

AFTER JESUS DOES the amazing miracle of feeding over five thousand people, He dismisses His disciples to cross the lake in a boat. Jesus wanted some time alone to pray so He told His disciples to get on a boat and go to the other side of the Sea of Galilee. The disciples encountered a storm and had been battling the weather for many hours. When Jesus approached them between 3 am and 6 am, they were physically exhausted. When the disciples saw Him, walking on water, they thought they saw a ghost.

Some scholars have tried to provide a natural explanation to the story like Jesus was actually walking on large rocks, just below the water, or bad weather inhibited vision and Jesus was actually walking along the shore. Others have said that it never happened and that the story is actually an allegory to show that only Jesus could rise above the storms of life, and if others would follow Him, they, too, would rise above the storm.

The story of Jesus walking on water must, however, be interpreted from a Jewish perspective. For first-century Jewish believers, it was unquestionable that the God of the exodus empowered Jesus to walk on water. In this case, they would not question whether it was possible but whether it happened. In this story, we have a theophany (or a visible manifestation of God to humankind): Jesus reveals Himself to His disciples as a divine being.

Matthew writes, *"When evening came, he was there alone, but the boat by this time was a long way from the land beaten by the waves, for the wind was against them"* (Mt 14:23b-24). Jesus' miracle of walking on the sea was to come to the aid of the threatened disciples. At first the disciples had to contend with the beating waves, and then they became terrified by what they thought was a ghost. But in the midst of the storm, Jesus brings calm to their hearts by saying, *"Take heart; it is I. Do not be afraid"* (Mt14:27). Jesus' divine being becomes more explicit when Jesus spoke. "The Greek for "It is I", is *ego eimi*, and is more literally translated, "I AM." This expression recalls the language with which God of the Hebrew Bible identifies God's self (for example, Ex 3:14, Isa 41:4; 43:10; 47:8, 10).[22]

Not only can Jesus walk on water, but He can also empower others to do likewise. Peter then says, *"Lord, if it is you, command me to come to you on the water"* (Mt 14:28). In Matthew, this is the first time Peter is given a special voice and thus becomes a representative for all disciples (see also Mt 15:15; 16:16; 17:4; 18:21: 19:27; 26:33, 35). Peter's address to Jesus ("If it is you" Mt 14:28) parallels the expression, "I AM". Thus, it is not meant to signal that Peter is unsure whether it is Jesus (especially since Peter calls Jesus, "Lord" but to serve as the condition for the request: Since you can walk on water, then command me to come to you on the water as well.[23]

What sort of person wants to walk on the water in the middle of a dark windstorm? It is said that students under the tutelage of a rabbi would imitate their teachers so as to become like them. Perhaps Peter wanted to imitate His teacher. Here we see a common characteristic of Peter, openly reckless and impulsive. Was Peter's request courage or insanity or a little bit of both? Yet, Jesus said, *"Come"* (Mt 14:29).

Peter's short walk was indeed a triumph of faith. But when he took his eyes off Jesus, fear kicked in and he began to sink. Peter shouts, *"Lord, save me"* (Mt 14:30). The same Peter who told Jesus to go away because he is a sinful person, now calls to the Lord to save him. Peter initially showed faith but when he doubted, he began to sink. Jesus reached out and saved him. Matthew ends the story confirming both Jesus' divine ability (the calming of the winds), and the disciples' growing faith in their worship of the Lord (Mt 14:33).[24]

Ironically, walking on water does not ultimately increase our faith, only sinking does. Those who ask for miracles and receive them soon forget. But those who have doubted, experienced God's love and who are pulled out of the sea of doubt, never forget. Peter's story is our story. There are times when we struggle with our unworthiness to be in His presence. Then there are times when we struggle with the realities of a fallen world, and we cry out, "Lord save me!"

Matthew (Mt 14:22-33), Mark (Mk 6:45-52) and John (Jn 6:15-21) record the miracle of Jesus walking on the Sea of Galilee. However, Matthew includes two details that Mark and John do not: (1) Peter also walks on water when Jesus calls him out of the boat, and (2) the disciples all confess Jesus to be the "Son of God" (Mt 14:33) after seeing the miracle. Matthew also emphasises on Peter's leading role and his sometimes impulsive behaviour.

The confession of Jesus' deity is not present in the parallel accounts (Mk 6:45– 52; Jn 6: 15–21). Matthew records the first time that the disciples use the title 'Son of God' to address Jesus. It is uncertain just how much they truly understood, because Mark ends the story by saying, *"for they did not understand about the loaves, but their hearts were hardened"* (Mk 6:52). It was only at the resurrection that they fully perceived Jesus as the Messiah. The three accounts in the gospels are witness to their growing, yet imperfect understanding of Jesus' identity.

The faith we possess is a gift from God (Eph 2:8-10) and Jesus sustains and perfects it in us (Phil 1:6) until He returns. When Peter began to sink, he helplessly cried out to the Lord, *"Lord save me"*. Jesus gently rebuked Peter for his *'little faith'*. Peter's experience is a reminder that we too can have lapse of faith that will not lead to failure. The Lord is near to raise us back safely to our feet when we call to Him for help. Gradually, Peter will learn to grow more and more in the faith, and he will learn to become bolder and more confident in the Lord. Years later, after the ascension of Jesus, Peter and John will stand before the Council comprising people who had sentenced Jesus to death. Peter and John will speak with boldness and astonish everyone who perceived them to be uneducated, common men. *And they recognised that they had been with Jesus* (Acts 4:13).

Reflection

There are different seasons in our lives. There are seasons of joy and there are seasons of grieve. Our ability to weather the stormy seasons depends on whether we fix our eyes on Jesus or the things around us.

Peter showed great faith when he walked on water as long as he fixed his eyes on Jesus. While we cannot see Jesus now, we can see His Word, the Bible. *Faith comes from hearing, and hearing through the word of Christ* (Rm 10:17). Jesus is the Word (Jn 1:1, 14), so we can see Him in the Word. As Christians, we see Jesus with the eyes of faith, knowing that He lived a sinless life and died to reconcile us to God, and that He will never leave or forsake us, just as He promised.

Isaiah said, *"If you are not firm in faith, you will not be firm at all"* (Isa 7:9b). Is your faith firm enough to know that God will never leave or forsake you, regardless of the situation? How do you handle challenges to your faith? What would you say to someone who asked how he could increase his faith in God?

-6-
RELIGIOUS HYPOCRISY
(MATTHEW 15:1-20)

JESUS WAS IN Galilee when the scribes (writers of the law) and Pharisees (strict religious sect) came from Jerusalem (about 123 km away) to attack Jesus. Jesus and the disciples were accused of breaking the tradition of the elders by not washing their hands before eating. As part of their ceremonial purification before entering the temple, only priests were required to wash their hands (Ex 30:17-21; Lev 22:4-7). Pietist circles may have extended the ritual to ordinary Jews after the temple's destruction and the exiles' return.

Pharisees maintained control over the people by upholding their man-made laws. They had elevated their rules and traditions to the same level as God's Law. In what way can man-made rules be compared to God's commandments? As God has commanded us not to add to His commandments (Dt 4:2; 12:32), this is undoubtedly a greater sin.

These high-powered scribes and Pharisees were dispatched from Jerusalem to expose Jesus' and His disciples' faults. What happened? Jesus exposed their faults and sins for all to see. The crowds heard the awful truth about them! Jesus showed them up to be lawbreakers, hypocrites, and sinners. While the Pharisees and scribes were offended by what He said about them, they could not reply to Him or refute Him. Jesus spoke the truth about them with authority from God. Jesus made it clear that obedience to tradition made a person disobedient to the Word of God, proving the tradition false. *And he called the people to him and said to them, "Hear and understand: it is not what goes into the mouth that defiles a person, but what comes out of the mouth; this defiles a person"* (Mt 15:10-11).

The disciples were worried about the reaction of the Pharisees to the way that Jesus humiliated them. *"Do you know that the Pharisees were offended when they heard this saying?"* (Mt 15:13). Jesus was not bothered. Jesus had no time for hypocrisy, especially from people who professed to be righteous. He referred to them as rootless plants that were dying. He said that they were blind people leading blind people who were destined to fall into a ditch.

Peter said to Jesus, *"Explain the parable to us"* (Mt 15:15). By 'this parable', Peter was referring to Jesus saying, *"It is not what goes into the mouth that defiles a person, but what comes out of the mouth; this defiles a person"* (Mt 15:10). According to Jesus, all man-made religions, as well as their traditions, and the teachers who promote them, are ineffective at meeting the needs of people. Instead, Jesus taught that true defilement of a person before God comes from within. The external observance of the law can't make us pure. Instead, we must helplessly pray to God for His saving grace, begging that He will remove our defilement from us and make us pure in His sight.

Jesus' words in Matthew 15:10 do not constitute a "parable" at all. Instead, they constitute a clear, plainly spoken spiritual principle. Jesus expresses frustration that they could not tell the difference.

All the disciples, including Peter, were Jews. In their upbringing, they had been taught the laws of Moses by scribes and Pharisees. They had been raised under strict dietary rules and ceremonial washing traditions. Jesus' declaration contradicted everything they had been taught and was a radical departure from everything they had learned and practised.

In Acts 10, we are told about Peter being given a missionary call to go to the home of a Gentile to share the gospel with him. The Lord had to break him free of his rigid adherence to traditions of ceremonial cleanliness. The Lord put Peter in a trance and gave him a vision of a sheet descending from the sky. When the sheet opened up, it contained all kinds of unclean animals for the Jewish person not to eat. The Lord said, *"Rise, Peter; kill and eat"* (Acts 10:13). Peter argued with the Lord in this vision. The Lord had to tell Peter, *"What God has made clean you must not call common"* (Acts 10:15). Peter had to learn that from the Lord. Peter's response during that vision shows us what a struggle Jesus' words must have presented to him concerning the tradition of ceremonial washing.

Reflection

It is important not to allow our words and actions to become ritualistic. Such words and actions can easily become hypocritical acts of worship. Jesus warned against religious hypocrisy with the strongest words because of its great danger. God wants more than just outward conformity; He wants a heart that responds and a mind that understands His commands. We must ensure that there is always inward devotion to God in our worship. Empty and hypocritical worship is intolerable to God. Our worship can become a ritual or a habit, but God wants worship that comes from the heart.

Are you at church to experience the presence of God, express your love to Him, and hear Him speak to you, or are you there because it's your usual routine on Sunday mornings? Someone once told me that Sunday is not Sunday if you do not go to church. Is that how you feel about Sunday and church?

Do you attend Bible Study regularly? If so, what is the reason? Did you join to fit in with the other Christians? Did you join because it is expected of you? Did you join because you wanted to know God better and deeper? Did you join to increase your Bible knowledge?

What is your real reason for attending church and Bible study?

-7-
STUMBLING BLOCK
(MATTHEW 16:13-23)

THE DISCIPLES HAVE been together for some two years now. The cross is a little more than six months away. Matthew 16 marks a turning point in the gospel (as evidenced by Mt 16:21-*From that time Jesus began to show his disciples ...*). For the first time Jesus mentions the church (Mt 16:18), and openly speaks about His death on the cross (Mt 16:21). He begins to prepare His disciples for His arrest, crucifixion, and resurrection. But as we shall see, they were slow to understand.

The parallel passages are Mark 8:27-30 and Luke 9:18-21. We will focus on the text in Matthew because Mark and Luke are very brief and only contribute some information to our understanding of what occurs.

Matthew 16 begins with a test from the religious leaders, two opposing groups united against Jesus, the Pharisees and the Sadducees (Mt 16:1-4). They ask Jesus to give them a sign from heaven. Jesus criticises them for their lack of spiritual insight. Rather than seeking a sign from heaven, the Pharisees and Sadducees should have recognised that the kingdom of heaven was already upon them.

Next, Jesus warns His disciples to beware of the *leaven of the Pharisees and Sadducees* (Mt 16:6), referring to the leaders' teaching and influence. But the disciples did not recognise the spiritual principle, and this seemed to have surprised Jesus Himself (*"Do you not yet perceive…"* – Mt 16:9a).

The Pharisees and the religious leaders had come all the way from Jerusalem to Galilee to seek Jesus. Matthew 16:4 says that after talking with them, Jesus *left them and went away* (Mt 16:4), presumably to get away from them. Jesus then took His disciples to the region of Caesarea Philippi, a Gentile territory in the north of Israel, about 120 miles from Jerusalem, and 25 miles north of the Sea of Galilee. Caesarea Philippi was scattered with temples of the ancient Syrian Baal worship. It was also the home of the cave temple of the great god Pan. The cavern was claimed to be the birthplace of Pan, the god of nature. The underground water at the back of the cave flowed out of the cave and fed the Jordan River. Alexander the Great was so impressed by the place that the Greeks built a shrine there to the god, Pan. The underground stream in the cave was so deep that it was considered bottomless.

The Romans were heavily influenced by the Greeks, and they followed many of their religious traditions, including the worship of Pan. In honour of the Roman emperor, Herod the Great built the temple of Augustus in front of the cave.[25] People or animals were sacrificed to Pan by throwing them into the deep underground stream. If the sacrificial victim disappeared into the waters, this was a sign that the sacrifice was accepted. If signs of blood appeared in nearby springs, however, it was believed the sacrifice had been rejected. The ancients believed that water symbolised the abyss and that caves were doors to the underworld. So, the cave temple could have represented the gates of Hades. It was in the midst of this pagan superstition that Peter confessed Jesus as the Son of God.

This brings us to Matthew 16:13-28. For the first and perhaps the only time in the Synoptic Gospels[26], Jesus shows an interest in what people think about Him. He asks the disciples, and they report current opinions. Then Jesus asks His disciples, *"Who do people say that the Son of Man is?"* (Mt 16:13). After they had given their responses, He then asked them (Mt 16:15), *"Who do you say I am?"* I believed the disciples must have discussed the reply among themselves first as they did in Matthew 16:7 (*And they began discussing it among themselves, ...*). Simon Peter, clearly the leader of the group answered on behalf them, *"You are the Messiah, the Son of the Living God"* (Mt 16:16). Jesus then tells Peter that the answer he gave is not from human wisdom or from Peter's own investigation but was revealed to him by His Father who is in heaven (cf. Mt 11:25-27). We will never be able to understand spiritual truths unless the Spirit opens our understanding (cf. 1 Cor 2:12-14). Only in the Holy Spirit can we truly confess that Jesus is Lord (1 Cor 12:3). Left to ourselves, no man, woman, or child can know God by simply applying our human reason or natural intuition. No one knows the things of God except by revelation of the Spirit of God.

Jesus then went on to explain the meaning of the title He gave Peter when He first laid eyes on him (Jn 1:42). Jesus said, *"And I tell you, you are Peter* [Gr. *petros* , meaning 'stone'], *and on this rock* [Gr. *petra* meaning 'rock'] *I will build my church, and the gates of hell* [Gr. the gates of Hades] *shall not prevail against it. I will give you the keys of the kingdom of heaven, and whatever you bind on earth shall be bound in heaven, and whatever you loose on earth shall be loosed in heaven"* (Mt 16:18-19).

What did Jesus mean when He said, *"And I tell you, you are Peter* [Gr. petros], *and on this rock* [Gr. petra] *I will build my church"?* Jesus was praising Peter for his accurate statement about Him, and was introducing His work of building the church on Himself. Consider the following verses:

> *So then you are no longer strangers and aliens, but you are fellow citizens with the saints and members of the household of God, built on the foundation of the apostles and prophets, Christ Jesus himself being the cornerstone,* - Eph 20:18-20

> *For no one can lay a foundation other than that which is laid, which is Jesus Christ.* – 1 Cor 3:11

The Lord builds the church on the truth of Himself, of which He is the chief cornerstone. And because the apostles through Peter were the first to testify to the truth, they were the foundation of His church and they bore witness to the truth throughout their ministries. In years to come, Peter will tell believers, *"you yourselves like living stones are being built up as a spiritual house, to be a holy priesthood, to offer spiritual sacrifices acceptable to God through Jesus Christ"* (1 Pt 3:5). Peter, by his own testimony about Jesus, can be seen as the first stone among many stones.

When Jesus said, *"and the gates of Hell (Gr. Hades) shall not prevail against it"*, Jesus was offering a promise that the forces of evil and darkness will never prevail against or conquer the church. By His death and resurrection, Jesus would conquer death, and death will lose its grip over His people. When Jesus mentioned gates of Hades, it resonated with the cave that represented the gates of Hades in Caesarea Philippi and so Jesus was also probably challenging the well-established pagan worship in Caesarea Philippi.

Jesus goes on to say, *"I will give you the keys of the kingdom of heaven, and whatever you bind on earth shall be bound in heaven, and whatever you loose on earth shall be loosed in heaven"* (Mt 16:19).

Key is a symbol of authority (Is 22:15, 22; Lk 11:52). 'Bind' and 'loose" were common Jewish phrases used by great Rabbis and great teachers. To bind something was to declare it forbidden. To loose something was to declare it allowed. These were used especially in doctrinal decisions.[27] Peter and the apostles were given the authority to represent Jesus, and through faithful proclamation of the gospel, they will open the door of the kingdom to those who respond in faith, while at the same time keeping it shut from those who do not.

What made Peter's confession so important was the fact that it came against the backdrop of all the confusion and false accusations about Jesus. His confession of faith was so strong that Jesus could begin talking about His death on the cross. He would go to Jerusalem, suffer and die, and be raised from the dead.

While Peter acknowledged Christ as the Messiah, he still had a different idea what the Messiah would do. Peter blurts out, *"This shall never happen to you"* (Mt. 16:22). In Jewish eschatology, the Messiah is a future Jewish king from the Davidic line and the future redeemer of the Jewish people. The Israelis expected the Messiah to inflict suffering and death on their enemies and on the wicked within Israel rather than experience it Himself. In this context, the disciples were not prepared for the idea that Israel's eschatological champion, the Davidic Messiah, would die a humiliating death. (In later years, the apostle Paul would preach in 1 Corinthians 1:23, *"but we preach Christ crucified, a stumbling block to Jews and folly to Gentiles."*)

Memories of Satan tempting Jesus in the desert might have come flooding back to Jesus. Satan tried to prevent

Jesus from carrying out what He had come to do. Now Peter is tempting Jesus to stumble in His perfect obedience to the Father. Jesus turned and said to Peter, *"Get behind me, Satan! You are a hindrance to me. For you are not setting your mind on the things of God, but on the things of man"* (Mt 16:23). In fact, the Greek word for hindrance is stumbling block. Simon was the rock and a stumbling block at the same time!

After this episode, Peter accepted Jesus' impending death on the cross and never questioned Him about it again. Jesus ends by saying, *"Truly, I say to you, there are some standing here who will not taste death until they see the Son of Man coming in his kingdom"* (Mt. 16:28). This statement will be fulfilled within a week at the Mount of Transfiguration, and this will be examined next.

Reflection
Peter was a stumbling block to Jesus when he tried stop Jesus from being crucified. Peter did *not set his mind on the things of God but on the things of man* (Mt 16:23).

Let me list three ways a Christian can be a stumbling block.

1. When you are called to a divine task, procrastination becomes a stumbling block to God's mission. By using you, God is blessing others and allowing them to enter His kingdom. Your procrastination would cause God's plan to be delayed or postponed.

2. In 1 Corinthians 8:9, Paul warns mature Christians not to use their freedom in Christ to dominate

weaker believers by claiming superior knowledge. The act of superiority can be a stumbling block for those growing in their faith. You should instead approach them with love for their edification.

3. Your walk with Christ is deeply personal, but it is also public. Christians publicly claim to uphold God's highest moral and spiritual standards. The media love to expose prominent Christian figures who fall into sin because of money, power, and sex, and the church must explain why they sinned. You become a stumbling block to those yet to hear the gospel if your lifestyle does not live up to the standards Christians claim to uphold.

Have your words and actions ever caused anyone to stumble? Was there any time in your life when you were told that something you did or said was unbecoming of a Christian? How did that make you feel?

-8-
LAW, PROPHETS AND THE MESSIAH
(MATTHEW 17:1-12)

THE TRANSFIGURATION IS covered in Matthew 17. Church tradition places the event on Mount Tabor because since the Byzantine period[28], Christians have been making pilgrimages to Mount Tabor to remember the miracle. Byzantine Christians have also erected churches and monasteries atop the hill.

However, gospel scholars seem to think it could be along the slopes of the lofty Mt. Hermon where the city of Caesarea Philippi is at its base. Mount Tabor is situated some fifty miles away from Caesarea Philippi. The event took place some six days after Peter's confession. Also, Matthew 17:1 says that Jesus led them to a 'high mountain', and Mount Hermon is the highest peak in Israel.[29] So scholars suggest the heights of Mount Hermon as the most likely candidate for the location.

At first glance, this event seems to be out of place. How does this event be connected with Jesus' mission? To understand the connection and to show it is not some random event recorded by the apostles, let us revisit the events that have happened so far.

It started with the disciples accompanying Jesus all over Galilee observing His power at work and listening to His teaching. John ends his Gospel by saying, *"Now Jesus did many other signs in the presence of the disciples, which are not written in this book; but these are written so that you may believe that Jesus is the Christ, the Son of God, and that by believing you may have life in his name"* (Jn 20:30-31). Jesus wanted His disciples to identify Him correctly, not as just another prophet but as the Son of God.

The disciples reached this plateau in Matthew 16, with Peter's confession. Let us recall the events. Jesus asked the disciples how the public perceived Him (Mt 16:13). The public response had been that Jesus must be one of the great prophets of Israel who has returned (Mt 16:14). Then Jesus asked how His disciples perceived him. Having witnessed Jesus of Nazareth's ministry unfold, Peter realises he is seeing more than just a gifted teacher, and declares Jesus to be the Christ. Jesus is deeply moved by the confession and commends Peter for it (Mt 16:17).

Jesus then announces, for the first time, His death and resurrection after Peter's confession (Mt 16:21). Jesus clashed head-on with the disciples' popular idea of Messiah. The popular idea involved a Messiah who came to earthly glory in victory over the Jews' enemies. For this reason, the Pharisees and Sadducees demanded a sign from Him (Mt 16:1) to confirm His messiahship. The people tried to take Jesus by force to make Him king, after He fed the five thousand (Jn 6:15) because feeding them was a messianic expectation (Ez 34:23-24).

Jesus, now acknowledged as Messiah, tells His disciples that He will, in effect, be the opposite of what they expected. He announces that He must go to Jerusalem and suffer many things from the elders and chief priests and scribes, and be killed. It is no wonder that Peter reacted the way He did (Mt 16:22). Peter could not imagine the Messiah dying at the hands of His enemies. Jesus rebukes Peter sharply for not accepting the idea of His death and resurrection. He even goes on to explain that not only will He die, but they too should be prepared to die in order to follow Jesus (Mt 16:24). It is in this context of confusion among the disciples that brings us to the Transfiguration story.

In Matthew 17, after 6 days, Jesus takes Peter, James, and John up on a high mountain. When they are all alone, something utterly astonishing occurs. A sudden appearance of glory is given to Jesus by God, *"And he was transfigured before them, and his face shone like the sun, and his clothes became white as light"* (Mt 17:2). Then there appeared Moses and Elijah. Together they represented the Law and the Prophets, both of which pointed to Jesus (cf. Rm 3:21).

In the excitement of seeing Jesus in His glorified state, and talking to Moses and Elijah, Peter, not knowing what he was saying and being very fearful, offered to put up three shelters for them. Despite Peter's good intentions, the specific action he suggested missed the point. The gospel portrays Peter as a man of extremes. While he has the faith and boldness to walk on water like Jesus, he also has the weakness of seeing the waves and sinking in them (Mt 14:28-31). Although he accurately asserts Jesus is the Christ, the Son of the living God, he receives a harsh rebuke for trying to derail Jesus from His divine mission (Mt 16:13-19, 21-23). The boldness and enthusiasm of Peter repeatedly reveal both a good heart and a reckless nature. In this particular situation, Peter made the mistake of making Jesus equal to Moses and Elijah. The voice of God the Father from heaven instructs Peter to listen to His beloved Son, "*This is my beloved Son, with whom I am well pleased; listen to him*" (Mt 17:5). The Father will not permit His beloved Son to be put on the same level as Moses and Elijah. *Jesus only* (Mt 17:8) is pre-eminent.

The Transfiguration confirmed Jesus' prediction in Matthew 16:28.[30] It also served to confirm Peter's confession. First, God shows the disciples a glimpse of Jesus' true heavenly glory. Then God reveals His heart for the Son by saying two things: "I love my son" ("*This is my beloved Son*"), and "My pleasure is in Him" ("*with whom I am well pleased*"). The Transfiguration demonstrated to Peter, James, and John that Jesus was not an ordinary man but that He was the Messiah, the Son of God. Peter never forgot what he witnessed because he mentions it in 2 Peter 1:16-21.

In Luke's version, Jesus spoke with Moses and Elijah about His approaching death in Jerusalem (Lk 9:31). It would only be through His death and resurrection that He would attain glory. Jesus' Transfiguration was not a random event but a perfectly timed and executed manifestation of glory that served to teach the disciples what kind of Messiah Jesus was and how He would attain greatness.[31]

Reflection

Jesus' Transfiguration demonstrated His divine nature and His glory, which He possessed before coming to earth in a human body. It was shocking for the disciples to hear Him talk about dying, and they began to wonder if He was really the Messiah. Peter, John, and James were taken to the top of a mountain by Jesus. In a fleeting moment, Jesus pulled back the veil of heaven and revealed His glory. The Transfiguration showed that Jesus' suffering is not incompatible with His glory.

As events unfold in this world, Jesus remains seated at our Father's right hand, moving everything forward to accomplish His purpose. We should all be encouraged by that. So, in the days ahead, let us live with glory in mind. We have something to look forward to as we await Jesus' return.

Considering that Jesus is coming soon, how should you live?

–9–
HOOK AND LINE FOR A SHEKEL
(MATTHEW 17:22-27)

AFTER THE TRANSFIGURATION, Jesus returns to Galilee (Mt 17:22) and heads for Capernaum (Mt 17:24). We will now examine Peter's encounter with the tax authorities concerning temple tax. This story is only recorded in the Gospel according to Matthew, who was himself, a tax collector.

Jerusalem's temple was a costly place to run. According to Exodus 30:13, every male Jew over twenty years of age must pay the half-shekel temple tax annually.

The tax authorities came to Peter and asked him if his Master paid His temple tax (half-shekel or two drachmas in Greek). The question may have been asked maliciously with the hope that Jesus would refuse to pay. If He refused, the collectors would have a basis for accusing Him.

Peter's immediate answer was that Jesus did pay. After entering the house, and before Peter could say anything to Jesus, Jesus asked Peter about taxation, and affirmed that just as the son of a king is exempted from paying taxes, He too was exempted from paying taxes because He was the Son of the King, the Son of God. However, Jesus agrees to pay the tax despite being free from that obligation. He does this to avoid causing unnecessary offense over this issue. Also, Jesus knows that the religious leaders are looking for anything they can use to discredit or arrest Him. He is not willing to make this issue a point of conflict.

Jesus commands Peter to find the money for the tax in a surprising way. He tells the former fisherman to go to the nearby Sea of Galilee, cast a hook, instead of a net, and catch a fish. In that fish's mouth, Jesus says, Peter will find a shekel. Peter was to use that coin to pay the tax for both him and Jesus. What are the chances of catching a fish that has retained a dropped shekel in its mouth and then takes a bite on Peter's hook with the shekel still in its mouth? The miracle is beyond comprehension when we consider its complexity - it's too complex to be coincidental. Think about a time when the Holy Spirit has done something beyond your comprehension. There have probably been times when you have been surprised at how God has come through for you in unexpected ways.

The irony of this story is that the Son of God was too poor to pay half-shekel. But as a demonstration of His kingship over nature, Jesus told Peter exactly what to do to get the money to pay the taxes for Jesus and himself.

Interestingly, there was no need to pay for the other disciples. Perhaps, among the disciples, only Peter was old enough to pay taxes.

Peter, as a fisherman, would use his net for fishing. But he obeyed Jesus' instruction and used a line to fish. (The Bible is silent, but we can assume he did obey Jesus.) Jesus tested Peter's faith when He told him how to catch the fish, which was his area of expertise. Our skills and talents often keep us from relying on the Lord. From Peter, we can learn that we should obey God, even if the instructions we receive seem contrary to our own better judgement.

This miracle was one of many miracles that Jesus performed for Peter. He healed Peter's mother-in-law (Mt 8:14-15), helped him catch a lot of fish (Lk 5:1-9), enabled him to walk on water (Mt 14:22-33), and now this. Peter could see that Jesus had Messianic powers. God had declared Jesus His Son clearly in the Transfiguration (Mt. 17:5). Also, Jesus accepted Peter calling Him the Messiah. Yet, the disciples had problems grasping that Jesus would resurrect after being killed. In Matthew 17:22-23, when Jesus told the disciplines about His impending death and resurrection, they were filled with grief. Mark says, *"But they did not understand what he meant and were afraid to ask him about it"* (Mk 9:32).

It's tempting to scoff at the disciples for their weak faith and ignorance. But we are no different. Like the disciples, we don't always understand what God is doing in our lives. We read God's clear promises in the Bible, yet often succumb to stress and doubt when life gets tough. Sometimes it isn't until after God has brought us through a trial that we can look back at Scripture and understand that He was with us from the beginning.

Reflection

Peter did some crazy things for Jesus, but it worked out! Jesus, a carpenter by trade, advised Peter to go fishing in the morning when his experience told him that was a crazy idea. Peter also went fishing with a hook and line rather than a net at Jesus' instructions.

Sometimes, God's instructions appear foolish, but that is because we are wise in our own eyes and believe we know better. God puts us in difficult situations or under trying conditions to help our faith to grow (see 1 Peter 6:7). George Muller said, "Faith does not operate in the realm of the possible. There is no glory for God in that which is humanly possible. Faith begins where man's power ends."

Imagine that you are holding a respectable position at work and earning a good salary. You are then called by God to take a job in a less developed country with a lower income and to work with a local church on a long-term project that requires your expertise. What would you do? You talk to a few people about it. Your colleagues at work think it's foolish to leave your current job. A Christian friend at church hands you a verse from Scripture that reads: *Trust in the Lord with all your heart, and lean not in your understanding* (Pr 3:5). Family members advise you to hold off on deciding for a few more years. Spend some time reflecting on your struggle with faith and fear. What will be your initial doubts and fears? What will convince you to take this step of faith?

-10-
SELL YOUR POSSESSIONS
(MATTHEW 19:16-30)

THERE IS A story of a rich young man who asked Jesus in Matthew 19:16, *"Teacher, what good deed must I do to have eternal life?"* Each of the first three gospels cover this event (Mt 19:16-23, Mk 10:17-22, and Lk 18:18-23). When we combine the facts, we learn that this young man was rich and a ruler, probably of a synagogue. Mark 10:17 also states that the man *"ran up to him"* and *"fell on his knees before him."* The young man was probably sincerely seeking an answer, but his approach to salvation was centred on works and not faith.

The young man asks Jesus, *"What good deed must I do to have eternal life?"* Jesus tells him to keep the commandments, and he responds that he has done that from his youth. The young man then asks Jesus, *"What do I still lack?"* Mark mentions that Jesus looked at him, and loved him (Mk 10:21). Jesus recognises in the young man before Him a fine, religious, good-living decent citizen, perhaps the kind of person who is a credit to any community. Jesus responds, *"Sell your possessions and give the money to the poor, and you will have treasure in heaven; then come, follow me"* (Mt 19:21).

The challenge was radical because of his strong attachment to wealth (Mt 19:22). God knows precisely what is in our hearts and what is needed as we serve Him. The rich young man wanted to know what to do to guarantee eternal life. He thought he could earn his way into the kingdom of heaven by obeying the law. The response of Jesus was intended to probe his righteousness; did he follow only the letter of the law or also the spirit? It was also to show him the true way to eternal life. By instructing the man to sell everything and follow Christ, the message was intended to reveal that he treasured his earthly possessions more than his heavenly hope and that he preferred to maintain his lifestyle than become a follower of Christ.

Now we come to the second part of the story where Jesus explains to the disciples what happened. When Jesus remarked that it would be easier for a camel to enter the eye of a needle than for a rich man to enter the Kingdom of God (Mt 19:23), the astonished disciples then asked who could be saved?

It went against the conventional thinking of the day. The Jewish people believed that riches were evidence of God's blessing. This was based on the promise God gave the Jewish nation at the beginning of their history. (See Dt 26-28.) God promised material blessings if they obeyed and material loss if they disobeyed. The disciples reasoned that since richness was a result of God's blessings then all rich people were guaranteed eternal life.

Jesus makes it clear that salvation is impossible apart from the work of God. For man to be saved, it is impossible to accomplish the goal on his own. God's unlimited power is needed to make the impossible, possible.

Then Peter speaks up (Mt 19:27) to remind Jesus that the disciples had left all and followed Christ, just as the Lord advised the rich young man. Surely, they are deserving to earn God's favour. In a way, Peter was asking, what would they get for following Jesus? Peter's response reflects the common notion that one must deserve or earn God's favour. He protested that they had left all, just as the Lord had advised the rich young man. What will they receive in return if they have made such a sacrifice?

Jesus tells of special honour for the disciples, *"Truly, I say to you, in the new world, when the Son of Man will sit on his glorious throne, you who have followed me will also sit on twelve thrones, judging the twelve tribes of Israel"* (Mt 19:28). In addition to everlasting life, there will be universal honour for all who sacrifice for Jesus' sake; whatever we give up for Him will be returned to us a hundred times over (Mt 19:29).

Very often, we observe Jesus correcting false beliefs and practices. We too must make sure we are obeying God in the manner that He wants us to. If we are lacking in knowledge of God's Word, we will struggle to fight against the enemy. Those who lack knowledge of God are easily swayed by the words of false teachers, who sugar-coat God's truth to win followers and exploit them. Without studying Scripture how are we to stand up to the lies of Satan? We saw how Satan tried to use Scripture to deceive Jesus when He was in the desert. But Jesus could not be deceived because He knew God's truth. How serious are you about studying the Bible?

Reflection

Anyone who believes he can earn a place in heaven by building up enough merit or good deeds is completely misinformed. Regardless of our actions, we will never earn or deserve a place in heaven. Jesus Christ is the only One who can save us. As our perfect substitute, He took the penalty of sin (2 Cor 5:21).

If someone told you that he believes that making every effort to be a good person is enough to get him a ticket to heaven, how would you respond?

How would you respond if someone told you he had difficulty accepting that he did not need to do anything to earn his salvation except by simply believing in Jesus Christ?

As soon as Peter realised his sinfulness, he obeyed Jesus and followed Him (Mt 4:9). In fact, he left everything for Jesus. However, unlike Peter, we tend to be indifferent about our encounters with Jesus. Why is that so? Why don't we feel the same passion for Jesus as Peter did? Why are we unwilling to give up everything, or at least to be ready and prepared to do so? Could it be that we have not really understood the depth of our depravity to comprehend the height of God's grace?

-11-
WASH YOUR FEET
(JOHN 13:1-20)

LET US CONSIDER the events before Jesus partook in the Passover with His disciples. After Jesus brought Lazarus back to life, the Jewish religious leaders in Jerusalem, jealous of His popularity, determined that Jesus must die and Lazarus too! (See Jn 11:47-53; 12:9-10.) When Jesus made His triumphal entry into Jerusalem, and after He cleansed the temple, the religious leaders began trying to discredit Him or get Him into trouble with the Roman authorities (Lk 20:19-20). Judas approached the chief priests to betray Jesus and he received an advance payment (Mt 26:14-16; Lk 22:1-6). Judas' offer delighted the chief priests. Now, all that remained was to wait for the right time to arrest Him. Judas wandered with Jesus for a good three years, *and as keeper of the money bag, he used to help himself to what was put into it* (Jn 2:6). Eventually, he decided that Jesus was not worth anything to him and betrayed Him for *thirty pieces of silver* (Mt 26:15). Judas used Jesus throughout the three years. He used Him again in the end.

And this brings us to John 13, the celebration of the Passover where Jesus washes the feet of His beloved disciples before He has His Last Supper with them. Let us examine the Last Supper covered in Matthew 26:17-30, Mark 14:12-26, Luke 22:7-38 and John 13:1-17, to understand the dining etiquette of that time in Israel.

Dining rooms called triclinia (*singular: triclinium*) have been discovered in ancient Roman houses.[32] The dining room has a couch for reclining at mealtimes, extending around three sides of the table. In most cases, the dining rooms faced the garden, providing a scenic backdrop for meals. It had long couches placed along three of its walls, hence its name. As they reclined on their left sides, their right hands were free to get food from the lower dining table in the center. By New Testament times, many Jews had adopted the Roman style of dining. The account of the Last Supper suggests that Jesus and the disciples were following this custom in a modified form. The home where they had the Passover would have been a wealthy home, as it had an upper chamber, and all of the preparations for the Passover feast would have already been made. (See Lk 22:9-13.)

The seating order was important.[33] That may be the reason why an argument arose among the disciples as to who was the greatest (Lk 22:24). The argument may have broken out because those who thought themselves to be the greatest lost out in the race for the chief seats. Peter, who was the oldest, and thus a likely candidate for "first chair", seems to have been more removed from Jesus than

John who was reclining on Jesus' side and who also may have been the youngest (Jn 13:23-25).[34]

Jesus and the disciples were not sitting but reclining and this is evident in Lk 22:14.[35] They would be reclining with their left elbow so that they would eat with their right hand, even if they were left-handed. This would mean that each guest could lean on the bosom of the person to their left. Their legs would be towards the outside, allowing a servant to wash their feet as they ate the feast.[36] Compare this with the scripture passage below:

And behold, a woman of the city, who was a sinner, when she learned that he was reclining at table in the Pharisee's house, brought an alabaster flask of ointment, and standing behind him at his feet, weeping, she began to wet his feet with her tears and wiped them with the hair of her head and kissed his feet and anointed them with the ointment.- Lk 7:37-38

The seating positions were from left to right. The host would sit second to the left, with the guest of honour on his left, and a trusted friend to his right. The seating then continued around the *triclinium*, the most important guests seated on the left, then going around the table, with the least important sitting on the far right. The servant, if seated at the table, would occupy the last position, closest to the door, so he could go and obtain more food as the evening progressed. The way the host honours his special guest is to dip bread into his bowl and put it in the mouth of the guest of honour, which is called offering the sop[37]. It was customary in Jesus' day to share the bowl of the host with the guest of honour. By understanding the culture, we can better understand what Jesus meant when He said:

"When you are invited by someone to a wedding feast, do not sit down in a place of honour, lest someone more distinguished than you be invited by him, and he who invited you both will come and say to you, 'Give your place to this person,' and then you will begin with shame to take the lowest place. But when you are invited, go and sit in the lowest place, so that when your host comes he may say to you, 'Friend, move up higher.' Then you will be honoured in the presence of all who sit at table with you. For everyone who exalts himself will be humbled, and he who humbles himself will be exalted." – Lk 14:8-11

If this seating arrangement was followed by Jesus, then Jn 13:23 indicates that John the beloved was seated to Jesus' right, as John had to lean on the bosom of Christ to ask of the identity of the betrayer. John 13:24 indicates that Peter was across from John, on the right side, as he had to signal to John to ask Jesus who would betray Him.

One of his disciples, whom Jesus loved, was reclining at table at Jesus' side, so Simon Peter motioned to him to ask Jesus of whom he was speaking. So that disciple, leaning back against Jesus, said to him, "Lord, who is it?" Jesus answered, "It is he to whom I will give this morsel of bread when I have dipped it." So when he had dipped the morsel, he gave it to Judas, the son of Simon Iscariot. – Jn 13:23-26

This would mean that the youngest apostle John was on the side of trust, while placing Peter, the one who is seen as the leader, was in the seat of the servant. One wonders if Peter was offended to end up in the servant's seat. And what would the disciples have thought about John, the youngest, having the seat of trust? Jesus being the teacher, took the opportunity to say this:

And he said to them, "The kings of the Gentiles exercise lordship over them, and those in authority over them are called benefactors. But not so with you. Rather, let the greatest among you become as the youngest, and the leader as one who serves. For who is the greater, one who reclines at table or one who serves? Is it not the one who reclines at table? But I am among you as the one who serves. – Mt 18:25-27

This seating arrangement would also mean that Jesus placed Judas, who would betray Him, in the seat of honour. Matthew 26:23 and John 13:26 indicate that Judas was seated to the left of Christ, in the seat of honour, as both Jesus and Judas were able to eat from the same bowl.

He answered, "He who has dipped his hand in the dish with me will betray me. – Mt 26:23

Jesus answered, "It is he to whom I will give this morsel of bread when I have dipped it." – Jn 13:26

It seems that to the very end Jesus loved Judas, and desired to teach him of His love by placing him in this most important seat. However, Judas had already made up his mind to betray Jesus.

Foot washing was needed in every home in Israel. The custom was to recline around the table at the evening meal. Servants were usually provided to wash the feet of guests, and it was a mark of honour for a host to provide a servant to wash a guest's feet. To fail to provide a servant was a breach of hospitality.

Then turning toward the woman he said to Simon, "Do you see this woman? I entered your house; you gave me no water for my feet, but she has wet my feet with her tears and wiped them with her hair. - Lk 7:44

So, to further teach Peter, and the others, the importance of servant-leadership, Jesus washed the feet of the twelve disciples, including Judas. The Jewish historian, Josephus, said that a free man acting as a servant was shameful.[38] Yet through this imagery of a servant washing feet, Jesus redefined greatness when He said, " *The greatest among you shall be your servant. Whoever exalts himself will be humbled, and whoever humbles himself will be exalted"* (Mt 23:11-12). Peter, who Jesus either placed in the position of a servant or had no choice but to take the last available seat, was most likely responsible for washing the feet of the guests. Yet, Jesus, the host and the greatest of them all, acted as a servant and washed their feet. Perhaps that was why Peter did not want Jesus to wash his feet. Yet Jesus insisted because Jesus always took the opportunity to teach a spiritual lesson when doing physical tasks.

Peter's first response to Jesus was to say that Jesus is too good to wash his feet. Jesus replies, *"If I do not wash you, you have no share with me"* (Jn 13:8). Peter had to accept this from Jesus. If we do not accept the sacrificial service of Jesus to cleanse us, we have no part with Him. Peter then went to say, *"Lord, not my feet only, but also my hands and my head!"* (Jn 13:9). Peter wanted to tell Jesus what to do, perhaps asking for a greater cleansing, demonstrating a desire to stand out from the crowd, Jesus replied, *"The one who has bathed does not need to wash, except for his feet, but is completely clean"* (Jn 13:10).

A new priest, consecrated for the first time to serve in the Temple, was washed from head to foot, and so baptised into the service of the sanctuary; but each time after that, when he went to offer sacrifice he washed his feet and his hands in the brazen laver.[39] Similarly, we need to be bathed in our trust in Jesus and what He did for us on the cross; that has been done once and for all. And we must continually wash our feet in faith and relationship with Jesus afterward.[40]

A lot of things that Jesus did may not have been immediately understood by the disciples. This prompted Jesus to say, *"What I am doing you do not understand now, but afterward you will understand"* (Jn 13:7).

Songwriter and author Michael Card, describes the moment beautifully: "This is a pivotal moment . . . in that Jesus finally gives up on words. He has told them numerous parables about slaves, now he will portray the most humiliating of slave roles, the washing of feet. Even after three long years of his often bizarre and indescribable behavior, the disciples are befuddled by the inappropriate behavior that leaves them speechless."[41]

Reflection

When Jesus washed His disciples' feet, it would have shocked them because they would not have expected their leader to do something like this. Jesus was teaching His disciples about the new way of life He would usher in through His death and resurrection. We are to emulate Him, serving one another in humility and love, seeking to build one another up as His followers. You are most like Jesus when you're serving others.

It is more important to God why you serve others than how well you serve them. Obeying God means doing what He has led you to do, and not what we want to do for Him.

Do you compare what you do for God's Kingdom with what others do? Do you ever feel that you need praise or recognition to motivate you to serve?

Is it important that what you do is visible to others? Are you willing to serve in areas unseen by others?

-12-
BITTER TEARS
(LUKE 22:31-34)

JESUS WARNED Simon Peter that a test of faith would come, *"Simon, Simon, Satan wants you so that he can sift you like wheat"* (Lk 22:31). The word *'you'* is plural in Greek. Satan's goal is to sift the disciples like wheat, to shake their faith so violently that they will fall. We see here a New Testament parallel to Job's story. Satan has made some holy arrangement with God. Jesus specifically prays and intercedes for Simon Peter. Jesus prays for Peter to recover from his failure, repent, turn around, and support his brothers to become a source of strength to them (Lk 22:32).

Satan wanted to destroy the disciples' faith and crush them. In fact, Satan seeks to destroy the faith of every believer (Jn 10:10). Jesus did not remove Peter's impending test. Instead, He predicted that Peter would fail the test by denying Christ three times (Lk 22:34). In our Christian lives, trials are to be expected, and *"through many tribulations, we must enter the kingdom of God"*

(Acts 14:22). Believers are allowed by God to be 'sifted' by Satan because faith is refined through suffering and trial. The more we rely on God, the more deeply we cherish His grace. God uses these experiences for our good (Rm 8:28), to refine our character and strengthen our faith (1 Pt 1:6-7; Jm 1:2-4,12), and to make us more like Jesus (Rm 8:29). Jesus would do the same for Peter, even at this final hour before His arrest.

The Lord also allows us to suffer through experiences of testing so that we can grow in faith and be able to help others grow. Paul said, *"If we are afflicted, it is for your comfort and salvation; and if we are comforted, it is for your comfort, which you experience when you patiently endure the same sufferings that we suffer"* (2 Cor1:6).

Peter is being tested in this trial. Will he live up to his name and calling? He believes he is ready. When I was a student at Bible College, I met many young Christians who wanted to be full-time preachers or missionaries for the Lord. Sadly, a few of them dropped out, or graduated and took up secular jobs instead. They came in their own strength to study. They were confident in themselves. They wanted to serve God on their own terms. In the end they left on their own terms.

Psalm 127:1 says: *Unless the Lord builds the house, those who build it labour in vain. Unless the Lord watches over the city, the watchman stays awake in vain.* Everything we do requires a total dependence upon God, for without the Lord being in charge, all efforts will be frustrated, and all activities will be rendered unsuccessful. Peter's reply shows that he was overconfident, trusting in his own strength: *"Lord, I am ready to go with you both to prison and to death"* (Lk 22:33). But Jesus prophesies that before the rooster crows, Peter will deny Christ three times (Lk 22:34).

John 18:1-11 describes the arrest of Jesus in Gethsemane. When Jesus identified Himself as the great I AM (*"I am he"* – Jn 18:5), the soldiers and temple police who came to arrest Him, were knocked to the ground. The power that was released hit them so hard and so fast that they were on their backs before they knew what hit them! *And when those who were around him saw what would follow, they said, "Lord, shall we strike with the sword?" And one of them struck the servant of the high priest and cut off his right ear* (Lk 22:49-50). John 18:10 identifies Peter[42] as the one who struck the high priest's servant and cut off his right ear before Jesus could reply. Scholars believe Peter intended to do more harm than just slice off the ear. Peter probably aimed for the man's head but missed, swiping the man's ear by mistake. Jesus stopped Peter and did His last earthly miracle of healing the man's ear.

Then Jesus said to him, "Put your sword back into its place. For all who take the sword will perish by the sword. Do you think that I cannot appeal to my Father, and he will at once send me more than twelve legions of angels? But how then should the Scriptures be fulfilled, that it must be so?" – Mt 26:52-54

Peter must have seen it as an opportunity to show bravery and take advantage of the situation. As Peter attacked the men with his sword, he demonstrated that he still didn't understand what Jesus would do in the next twenty-four hours. We must admire the courage of Peter who would stand up to a group of soldiers experienced in killing men. He was hopelessly outnumbered and outmanned. But Jesus was teaching Peter to reject the sword and embrace the cross.

Jesus is taken to the house of the High Priest. Peter is warming himself beside a charcoal fire in the courtyard. Refer to Luke 22:54-62. While remaining incognito, Peter tries to stay close to Jesus. Despite his denials, his Galilean accent betrays him (Lk 22:59). While he was still speaking, denying Jesus for the third time, immediately, the rooster crowed. *And the Lord turned and looked at Peter. And Peter remembered the saying of the Lord, how he had said to him, "Before the rooster crows today, you will deny me three times"* (Lk 22:60b-61).

Exactly as Jesus predicted, Peter denied Jesus three times. Peter is the only disciple to betray Jesus publicly. The word Luke used for "look" is the same word John used when Jesus looked at Peter when He met him for the first time. It was a look of love and forgiveness that would have broken Peter. *And he* [Peter] *went out and wept bitterly* (Lk 22:62).

We are like Peter. When Jesus gazes at us, He sees our frailties, our faults and also our potential. He sees us at our best, and He sees us at our worst. And despite the numerous times we fail Him, He gazes at us with love and forgiveness and points to the cross. Paid in full.

Reflection

At the time of Jesus' crucifixion, Peter was afraid to confess his knowledge of Him. Peter messed up. Sometimes we mess up too. Have there been times when you were afraid to openly admit that you are a Christian? And did you hate yourself for feeling weak in comparison to the other Christians who seem to be able to speak boldly and fearlessly for Christ?

When Peter was afraid that he would drown during a stormy night, he cried to the Lord, and the Lord stretched out His hand and lifted him up (Mt. 14:30). Even after Peter denied Jesus three times, Jesus prepared a meal for him and reconciled with him (Jn 21:10-12). God knows our fears; He will not stop loving or caring for us. Ask Him how to overcome your fears, and He will guide you through His word or by sending others to help you.

Social media has accused Christians of being self-righteous, judgemental, unforgiving, unloving, intolerant, and bigoted. How would you respond to these accusations? Would you be afraid to admit that you are a follower of Christ, or will you stand up for Him despite ridicule?

-13-
BREAKFAST WITH JESUS
(JOHN 21:1-23)

WHEN MARY MAGDALENE saw the empty tomb (Jn 20:1-10), early in the morning, she assumed that the body had been taken away or stolen. She ran to inform Peter and John that the body had been taken away. Both Peter and John ran to the tomb. John being younger, outran Peter. He stooped to see the empty tomb but did not go in, until, Peter, his leader, went in to inspect the tomb. They both saw the burial wrappings that was used to wrap Jesus, lying in the tomb. If Jesus' body had indeed been stolen, there would be no time and no need to remove the linen from His body. John was convinced that Jesus had resurrected (Jn 20:8), but he and Peter did not yet understand that the Scriptures predicted the resurrection of the Messiah (Jn 20:9).

After the resurrection, Jesus appeared to His disciples a few times. Jesus appeared first to Peter and then the other disciples (Lk 24:34; 1 Cor 15:5). But Peter was still reeling from his denial of Christ. Not knowing what else to do, he went fishing (Jn 21:1-23). After a night of catching absolutely nothing, they met an unknown person on the shore in the early dawn, a man who asked about the catch and asked them to cast their net on the other side of the boat. They did so, and their nets were filled and overflowing with fish. And immediately they recognised their Lord. Something similar happened three years earlier when Jesus met them at the shore and gave Simon his new name. Peter recognised that the person was Jesus and quickly leaped overboard and began swimming towards shore. There was a charcoal fire and Jesus made breakfast for His disciples with the fish they caught.

As Peter sat beside the charcoal fire, the smell of the flames would have brought back memories when Peter was warming himself beside a charcoal fire in the courtyard of the house of the High Priest, and denied Jesus three times. Jesus asked Peter three times if he loved Him more than the other disciples. Peter had denied Jesus three times and now Jesus gave Peter three chances to declare his love – one for each denial. Jesus' response was to repeat the same invitation for Peter to follow Him, precisely the same invitation that had begun their relationship three years earlier.

In the past Peter was a loud, brash and direct, and perhaps intimidating. Here is a different scene. When Jesus prepared breakfast for them, Peter did not protest. When Jesus asked him if he loved Him, Peter did not protest that he loved Jesus more than any disciple. He knows Jesus can see a person's heart to the very core. Peter replied, *"Lord, you know everything; you know that I love you"* (Jn 21:17b).

In John 21:18-19, Jesus predicts that Peter would die by crucifixion. In an ironic way, it is also a prediction that Peter's restored faith would never fail again, even in the face of his own death. Jesus' last recorded words to Peter were *'follow me'* (Jn 21: 19, 22), the same words He said years earlier (Lk 5:1-11) to Peter, inviting him to be a fisher of men. In this passage, the command *'Follow me'* is a present imperative in the Greek text, which literally means 'Keep on following me.'

Peter had finally arrived at the point where Jesus could now use him. And so, he tells Peter to be a shepherd to His sheep, the followers of Jesus. In Luke 7:47, Jesus says that we know we have been forgiven for our sins, because it will be evident in our love for Christ. Peter's love must be the greatest since Jesus reconciled with him and commissioned him to feed His sheep. We should take hope from Peter's restoration story to such a prominent leadership position in the church that Jesus wants to restore us when we fall.

Reflection

When Peter saw Jesus on the seashore, he plunged into the water and raced towards Jesus. The weight of guilt for denying Jesus was heavy on him, but the sight of Jesus brought inexpressible joy to him.

Nothing steals joy like guilt. Unconfessed sin, or living in sin, causes a huge distance between you and God. What joy is there when you stand in His presence during prayer, worship, or communion when your life is wrecked by sin? All you feel is condemnation. Life will not feel joyful until we confess our sins and experience God's forgiveness.

A Christian confides in you that he has been struggling with a habitual sin. He was told by a Christian friend that God would reject him if he kept sinning willfully. He is worried. How would you respond?

You know of another person from your church who has been willfully indulging in pornography for a long time. He claims that Christ is his Saviour and since his past, present, and future sins have been forgiven, God's forgiveness allows him to continue sinning. How would you respond to him?

-14-
BE SOBER-MINDED

SOMEONE DESCRIBED PETER during Jesus' time as a bull in a China shop, that is, someone who bulldozed his way around and did whatever he thought was right, regardless of the consequences. It was always Peter who answered Jesus' questions or asked Him questions. He was headstrong and often spoke in haste. He sometimes told Jesus what to do and got rebuked for it.

Peter was assertive, focused, determined, and proactive, but his wisdom, strength, and self-confidence often hindered him and caused him to make mistakes. He was strong in spirit but weak in the flesh. Peter fell asleep while Jesus asked him to pray in the garden. After cutting off the ear of the slave of the High Priest, he went into hiding.

For Peter, great success in faith or action seemed to be followed by failure. After walking on water to Jesus, he lost sight of Jesus and sank. After declaring allegiance to Christ, he denied Him three times.

Peter also had his strengths too. Peter was excited to learn from Jesus and see what He did first-hand. His commitment to Christ was unwavering. He gave up his career and his home to follow and serve Christ. He was part of the inner circle of Jesus who witnessed the Transfiguration of Jesus. He was given a new name as the first of many living stones to build the church. He was commissioned to strengthen and nurture Jesus' flock.

In the days before he followed Jesus, Peter felt secure in his competence and self-reliance. His expertise as a fisherman in the Sea of Galilee and his courage were the sources of his confidence. Peter knew everything there was to know about fishing and handling the rough sea, or so he thought. His self-confidence and self-reliance came tumbling down after he met Jesus. Let us briefly revisit how this happened.

In Luke 5:1-11, while teaching at the lake of Gennesaret[43] Jesus instructed Peter to lower the nets at the deep end for a catch. Peter protested to Jesus that after a futile night of fishing, it would be impossible to catch any fish during the day. However, Peter obeyed Jesus and cast his nets into the deep end. The catch was so huge that the nets began to break, and two boats were needed to fill the catch, almost sinking. Despite a futile night, there was an unprecedented catch of fish in an area that had seemed hopelessly unproductive. Jesus' powerful and authoritative words caused all of this to happen. Who is this man who commands the fish to be caught? In the presence of Jesus,

Peter recognises his unworthiness, and he confesses his sinfulness to Jesus (Lk 5:8).

In Mark 4:11-22, we read about Jesus calming the storm. A terrible storm arose. High waves began to break into the boat until it was nearly full of water and about to sink. Even Peter and the other fishermen in the boat feared for their lives. At this point, all their knowledge and experience in handling the rough seas seemed to have reached their limit. They awoke Jesus who immediately calmed the storm. Who was this man who could control nature? Peter and the others were filled in awe.

In Matthew 17:22-27, Jesus instructs Peter to find the tax money in a surprising way. The former fisherman is told to cast a hook instead of a net at the nearby Sea of Galilee and catch a fish. Jesus told Peter that he will find a shekel in the mouth of that fish. How likely is it that Peter will catch a fish that swallows a dropped shekel with the shekel still in its mouth when the fish bites Peter's hook? This is too much to comprehend, even for a fisherman.

Over time, Peter began to trust in Christ's sufficiency instead of his own. This led Peter to confess, *"Lord, you know everything"* (Jn 21:17). Jesus stripped Peter of his earthly identity as a fisherman and equipped him to live as God had called him to be, a fisher of men. This led Peter to say, *"His divine power has granted to us all things that pertain to life and godliness, through the knowledge of him who called us to his own glory and excellence"* (2 Pt 1:3).

The man who thought that he should keep a checklist or scorecard on how many times he forgives a brother who sins (Mt 18:21-22) learned from Jesus that *love covers a multitude of sins* (1 Pt 4:8).

The man who fell asleep instead of keeping vigil and praying with Jesus at Gethsemane instructs us to be *"self-controlled and sober-minded for the sake of your prayers"* (1 Pt 4:7).

The man who remained seated as Jesus washed the disciples' feet now calls us to *"eagerly"* serve the Lord (1 Pt 5:2).

The man who sliced off the ear of the High Priest's servant at the garden tells us: *"Submit yourselves for the Lord's sake to every human authority"* (1 Pt 2:13, NIV).

The man who argued with the disciples about who was the greatest in the kingdom of heaven tells us, *"Humble yourselves, therefore, under God's mighty hand, that he may lift you in due time."* (1 Pt. 5:6).

The man who witnessed Jesus' symbolic act of servant leadership when Jesus washed his feet, served alongside the other elders among the exiled Christians in Asia Minor as a *"fellow elder"* (1 Pt. 5:1), even though he held a special position among the disciples.

The man who remembered Jesus telling him how Satan asked for Peter's faith to be sifted as wheat, but

Jesus prayed that Peter's faith would not fail, tells us, *"Be alert, for the devil prowls around looking for someone to devour. Resist him, standing firm in the faith, because you know that the family of believers throughout the world is undergoing the same kind of sufferings"* (1 Pt.5:8-9).

Peter's life is perhaps the greatest redemption story ever recorded. Even though Peter denied Jesus at a critical moment in Jesus' life, Peter later suffered beatings, imprisonment, and eventually death rather than deny Jesus again. It takes time to develop such a character. Over three years, Jesus patiently transformed Peter, teaching, admonishing, serving, forgiving, and loving him. In years to come, Peter will pen down the following in his first letter (1 Peter) to the exiled Christians in Asia Minor, *"Like newborn infants, long for the pure spiritual milk[44], that by it you may grow up into salvation"* (1 Pt 2:2). Peter realised time spent with Jesus produces maturity in the believer's relationship as it had for him.

Peter, who we read about in the four gospels, became Peter, who we read about in Acts, and, who wrote two epistles. His discipleship with Jesus and the outpouring of the Holy Spirit he received at Pentecost transformed Peter into an outstanding leader. Peter's story is recorded so we can hope for God to do the same in our lives. The life of Peter is a testament to the fact that we can change! From frustration and failure, we can move towards fulfillment and fruitfulness. It is God's intention for our lives and our inheritance.

Reflection

Through Christ, God cleanses us of all unrighteousness by taking our sins away. Every day He works on us to make us what He needs us to be. As you reflect on your own life, how has God transformed you?

Jesus said to him, *"No one who puts his hand to the plough and looks back is fit for the kingdom of God"* (Lk 9:62). 'Hands on the plough' is a proverbial expression that signifies beginning a new endeavour. In this case, a person who puts his hands on the plough is committing his life to God. As a Christian, it is our responsibility to bear much fruit. Looking back will prevent us from ploughing our fields properly, resulting in a bad harvest.

We must never return to this world after responding to God's call out of this world. Yet, because of the many pleasures this world can offer - the lust of the flesh, the lust of the eyes, and the pride of life, we can be tempted to look back. When this happens, we are preventing ourselves from bearing much fruit.

Have you struggled with looking back? Has this struggle affected or slowed down your transformation in Christ? How would you advise a young Christian to keep his hands firmly on the plough?

-15-
No Shortcuts

ONE THING we can identify with Peter is his failures. Peter was bold and passionate about following Jesus, but sometimes his rash words or impulsive actions got him into trouble. This seemed to be part of his nature even after the Spirit was given at Pentecost.[45] Haven't we had similar experiences too? We can be on fire for God and then in a moment of weakness, we say or do something that put us to shame as Christians.

Peter was the boldest of all the disciples. He said things that other disciples only thought. For example, in Matthew 19:27, Peter told Jesus that the disciples left everything to follow Him and asked what they would get from doing so. Some scholars felt that Peter was out of line for asking this question, while others thought it was a question that needed to be answered especially for those who left everything for Jesus; their home, their family, their career. In His reply (Mt 19:28-30), Jesus told them that the apostles are promised a spectacular reward. Jesus went on to say that anyone who made sacrifices for Jesus would be rewarded. However, Jesus added, *"But many who are first will be last, and the last first"* (Mt 19:30). Jesus illustrates this point in the parable of the workers in the vineyard in the chapter that follows (Mt 20). In the parable, the right attitude toward service is emphasised. The rewards we receive are not based on our merits but on God's grace and generosity. Our service to God should not be motivated by the expectation of receiving a reward. We will always receive better than we deserve from God because He is infinitely generous and gracious.

Do you ever wonder if your regular attendance at church or Bible study classes might earn you God's favour? God already loves you. He loves you deeply and fully. Attending church or studying the Bible is not to gain favor with God but to understand and recognise His love and grow in our relationship with Him. In fact, regular Bible study classes can help you gain a deeper understanding of God. A deeper understanding of God's love and mercy should, in turn, motivate us to offer ourselves unconditionally as living sacrifices and to serve Him lovingly wherever God calls us. You should re-evaluate your reason for attending Bible Study classes if you are not motivated to offer yourself as a living sacrifice for His service.

Peter was the kind of person who dared to do things that others would not. In Matthew 14:22-27, Peter asked Jesus to command him to come to Him on the water. As long as Peter focused on Jesus, he could walk on water, but as soon as he turned his attention to the stormy waves, he almost drowned. Faith will unleash the supernatural, but fear will cause us to sink. When fear struck, Peter called out to his Master, *"Lord, save me!"* It is so comforting to know that even when we are weak in faith, we can call out to Jesus, and He is always a helping hand away.

There is an earlier storm scene in Matthew 8:23-27, where Jesus gets up from sleep in the boat and calms the storm. Like Jesus during a violent storm, we can rest in God during life's storms. When we rest in God, we must trust Him no matter what our circumstances are. If trials, hard times, and disappointments threaten to shipwreck your faith, remember the words of Jesus who speaks to you:

"Why are you afraid, O you of little faith?" (Mt 8:26a)
"O you of little faith, why did you doubt?" (Mt 14:31b).

In Mark 8:31-33, when Jesus told His disciples that He would suffer and die, Peter rebuked Him and tempted Him to take a shortcut so that He could avoid the horror of the cross. In our Christian lives, we sometimes seek shortcuts. But there are no shortcuts to heaven. There are no shortcuts to spiritual growth. There are no shortcuts to becoming a Christian. A lady once asked me if her son would be saved if she got him to recite the sinner's prayer[46]. I told her that there was no shortcut to salvation. Her duty as a Christian mother was to provide her son with a Christian upbringing, train him how he should go (Pr 8:22), and pray that he will make a personal commitment to accept Jesus Christ as his Lord and Saviour.

Many false teachers today offer 'shortcuts' to salvation and God's blessing. They have deceived many Christians into believing that they can get God's blessing for good health and great wealth by giving generously to these teachers.

Peter was unclear why Jesus had to suffer and die. His lack of understanding led him to offer Jesus an alternative to the cross. We can easily be deceived by false teachers when we do not understand God's word and accept their teaching instead. Peter warns us, *"Be sober-minded; be watchful. Your adversary the devil prowls around like a roaring lion, seeking someone to devour"* (1 Pt 5:8-9). Be diligent in studying Scripture so that you will not be deceived.

For three years, Peter followed Jesus and loved Him. He even swore he would die for Jesus. Then, on the night Jesus was arrested, Peter denied Him three times between midnight and daybreak. When rooster crowed at his third denial Jesus turned to face Peter. Peter went away and wept bitterly. Guilt, shame, and despair must have plagued Peter. He must have replayed the denial in his head over and over again. Even though Peter met Jesus a few times after His resurrection, there is no record that Peter ever discussed the denial. He may have felt guilty about bringing up the subject. Perhaps he even wondered if Jesus would ever forgive him. A broken relationship with Jesus, whom he loved and left everything for, was weighing him down.

In John 21, the disciples had been fishing all night, but by morning they had not caught anything. Then Jesus appeared and told them where to fish. Peter, upon recognising Jesus' voice (Jn 21:7), *put on his outer garment, for he was stripped for work, and threw himself into the sea.* Peter plunged into the sea to reach him first. I can only imagine how heartwarming it was for Jesus to see Peter race towards Him. Peter must have felt an inexpressible and glorious joy (cf. 1 Pt 1:8) to see his Lord and Master, who he betrayed some days earlier, inviting him and the disciples to breakfast! Peter loved Jesus and wanted to reconcile with Jesus. Jesus loved Peter and wanted to forgive him to restore the relationship. Here we have a beautiful picture of love and forgiveness. No wonder Peter said, *"Above all, keep loving one another earnestly, since love covers a multitude of sins"* (1 Pt 4:8).

It is common for us to hide from God when we sin. Satan whispers in our ears that we are failures and should give up seeking forgiveness because God has given up on us. We are burdened by guilt. We are embarrassed to seek forgiveness. We are weighed down by a broken relationship with God. What wonderful joy it is to know that Jesus is always knocking on the door of our hearts and waiting for us to open that door to Him. Like Peter, we too can receive forgiveness from the Lord even when we fail and sin, repent (1 Jn 1:9), and experience His love again.

Jesus knew Peter's failures, and He knows ours as well. As a result, we should be confident enough to move forward after failure. No failure or success in our life catches God by surprise. Even though God knew every detail of Peter's life, He still used him for His glory.

We may feel like we have failed God, that we cannot recover from the grievous errors of the past, but Peter teaches us that failure does not define us. God often uses the failures we experience to humble us, remind us of our limitations, make us more willing to depend on Him, submit to His commands, and remain open to His leadership in our lives.

Peter's life-transforming journey began when Jesus said, "*Follow me*". Peter left his nets to follow Jesus. It wasn't a smooth ride, and there were bumps along the way. After the resurrection, Jesus predicted that Peter would be crucified for His sake. Despite hearing about his death in graphic detail, Peter took comfort and joy in hearing that it would glorify God. Peter continued to love and honour Jesus throughout his ministry and life. In stark contrast to the man who once said he would lay down his life for Jesus and then denied Him, Peter's martyrdom showed the courage, faith, patience, and perseverance of a transformed man, who rejoiced to be counted worthy to die for Jesus' name,

How has your journey with God been? I am sure your journey is fraught with failures, just like mine. Yet God continues to love wretches like us. Such love is beyond comprehension. So let us persevere with God, seeking forgiveness when we sin, and allowing Him to transform us to become more like our Saviour, Jesus Christ.

Reflection

Recently, I was listening to a Christian song, which I felt sums up this study of Peter's journey with Jesus. I have added the final stanza for you to meditate on the words.

My heart is filled with thankfulness
To him who reigns above,
Whose wisdom is my perfect peace,
Whose ev'ry thought is love.
For ev'ry day I have on earth
Is given by the King;
So I will give my life, my all,
To love and follow him.

Song: My Heart is Filled with Thankfulness (3rd stanza)
Songwriters: Keith Getty / Stuart Townend

When Jesus met Peter and Andrew at the seashore, He called out to them. *Immediately they left their nets and followed him* (Mt 4:20). Three years passed. Peter told Jesus he left everything for Him (Mt 19:27-29). Then Peter's world turned upside down when he denied Jesus three times (Lk 22:54-62). Peter's heart was heavy. He decided to return to his old familiar, comfortable world, fishing (Jn 21:3). Another encounter with Jesus at the seashore was necessary to motivate him to continue following Him. It was Jesus who reached out to him and reconciled with him (Jn 21:15-19).

Procrastination, guilt feelings, busy lifestyle, worldly distractions, or wrong priorities can also cause us to gradually slip back into our familiar, comfortable surroundings. If that is the case for us, then we need another encounter with Jesus. Jesus never left us. He is there, waiting for us to invite Him back into our lives so that He can have fellowship with us. After all, Jesus said, *Behold, I stand at the door and knock. If anyone hears my voice and opens the door, I will come in to him and eat with him, and he with me* (Rev 3:20).

We are reaching the end of this book. In what ways have the Lord spoken to you through the book? Was there anything that touched, or impacted, you? Did the book inspire you to try something new or different, or to take on a challenge, or to change certain behaviours, or to do a complete makeover of your current lifestyle? It is my prayer that this book has been a blessing for you. In the words of Peter (2 Pt 3:18): *But grow in the grace and knowledge of our Lord and Savior Jesus Christ. To him be the glory both now and to the day of eternity. Amen.*

Epilogue

Peter became a different man when he received the Holy Spirit at Pentecost. He was empowered and emboldened. He never forgot the lessons learnt from his Master. Although he made mistakes along the way like all of us, God still used him mightily.

Peter was a pillar of the early church and one of its most influential leaders. The Bible has given us some interesting insights into Peter's life but not much about how he died. How did Peter die?

According to church tradition, Peter was crucified upside-down in Rome. Tradition says that Peter requested to be crucified on an inverted cross. He made this request because he didn't think he was worthy of dying as Jesus did. Again, this story is based on tradition, not on Scripture.

What we do know for sure about Peter's death is Jesus' prophecy in John 21:18–19: *"Truly, truly, I say to you, when you were young, you used to dress yourself and walk wherever you wanted, but when you are old, you will stretch out your hands, and another will dress you and carry you where you do not want to go." (This he said to show by what kind of death he was to glorify God.) And after saying this he said to him, "Follow me."' According to Jesus, Peter will glorify God through this kind of death.*

Jesus foretold Peter's death to prepare him for the difficulties he would face now that His Lord would no longer physically be with him after His ascension. 'Stretching out his hands' (cf. Jn 21:18) could be interpreted as Peter dying on a cross with his arms outstretched. No matter how he was executed, Peter was at the mercy of others who tied him and carried him to his death. Despite the gruesome details of Peter's death, he must have taken comfort and joy in hearing that it would glorify God (Jn 21:19). It is unclear what Peter's exact age was during his execution. According to ancient writers, Peter was executed 32 years after Jesus prophesied.

The love Peter had for Jesus and his desire to obey and glorify Him were evident throughout the rest of his life and ministry. The willingness of Peter to die a martyr's death testifies to his courage, faith, patience, and perseverance. He rejoiced to be counted worthy to die for Jesus' sake. Peter served the Lord Jesus because he loved Him. What is your reason for serving the Lord Jesus?

ABOUT THE AUTHOR

Andrew Sabaratnam (BSc Hons, MSc, MCS, PBM, PBS)

ANDREW SABARATNAM GRADUATED as an engineer and has been an educator for over 34 years. Andrew is also a Bible Scholar. He holds a Graduate Diploma in Christian Studies from Singapore Bible Studies and a Masters in Christian Studies from Biblical Graduate School of Theology, Singapore. His interests include Church History, Spiritual Classics of Christianity, Contemporary Issues and the Bible, Christian Biographies, God and the Movies, and Biblical Archaeology. Additionally, Andrew is a Cultural Intelligence certified trainer who conducts workshops for churches and mission organisations on reaching people from different cultures. Andrew is known for taking complex topics and making them easy to understand and palatable for everyone.

Other book in Amazon by Author
Ruins, Rubble and The Rock: Authenticating the Gospel Era with Archaeological Evidence

Other Books by Author
- A Helping Heart: A Counselling Manual for Volunteers
Andrew T. Sabaratnam, M.S. Poon

- Light for my Path
  Sabaratnam, Poon, Sabaratnam-Ang, Yap

ENDNOTES

1 Matthew 16:17 says that Peter is the son of Jonah; while John 1:42 and 21:15-17 says that he is the son of John. It is not known why the difference. One possibility is scribal error in John.

2 Over one hundred dialects of Aramaic were spoken in the Middle East in the first half of the twentieth century. The Jews adopted Aramaic when they were exiled to Mesopotamia in antiquity by the Babylonians, and some remained there. (Source: Institute Advanced Study-Aramaic and Endangered Languages)

3 Hellenism describes the influence of Greek culture on the conquered people of the Greek and Roman Empires.

4 This a Jewish coming of age ritual for boys.

5 David Bivins, *Jesus' Education*, www.jerusalemperspective.com, under "Articles."

6   Taken from the chapter "Education and the Study of Torah" by Safrai and Stern in *"The Jewish People in the First Century"*, Brill Academic Publishing, 1988

7   Thomas Nelson, For God So Loved the World – *John*, Impact Bible Study Series, Thomas Nelson, Inc, 2005 (See topic on "What Was It Like to be a Fisherman on the Sea of Galilee in Ancient Israel?")

8   Source: bibletools.org - *Temple Tax*

9   Strabo, Geography, XVI, 2,45

10 Source; Biblical Archaeology Society, August 9, 2016 – *The Fishy Secret to Ancient Magdalas Economic Growth*

11 Michael Grant, *Saint Peter*, Scribner, NY, USA, 1995, p.56

12 Strabo, Geography, XVI, 2,45

13 John 1:40 - *One of the two who heard John speak and followed Jesus was Andrew, Simon Peter's brother.* Andrew as one of the two disciples. Scholars believe that the other one was John the apostle himself, who never mentions his own name in his Gospel nor the name of any of his relatives.

14 Source: Website – Preserving Bibles Times. See Article on *Reflection: Follow Me.*

15 Source: Website - That the World May Know. See article on *Rabbi and Talmidim.*

16 Source: Bill Hunt, *The Complete Book of Discipleship: On Being and Making Followers of Christ,* Navpress, 2006.

17 John 1:42 is inferring here that Simon received the special name Cephas at his first meeting with Jesus, although Mt.16:16-18 mentions it later in its accounts. Scholars have provided possible reasons for this. One reason was that he (probably) got the name first in John 1:42 and he (probably) learned the reason for the name in Matthew 16:18.

18 Oscar Cullmann, *Peter,* SCM Press Ltd, London, 1953, p.20

19 Christopher Pain, *Towards an Understanding of Jesus' Relationship,* Jubilee Centre, Cambridge, UK, 2007, p.28

20 Evan Milton, *The Evidence for Jesus Resurrection, Part 2: How to Do History,* CrossExamined.org, 22 April 2021.

21 Elizabeth McNamer, *The Case for Bethsaida after Twenty Years of Digging: Understanding the Historical Jesus,* Cambridge Scholars Publishing, 2016, pp.44

22 O. Wesley Allen Jr, *Matthew,* Fortress Press, USA, 2013, pp.158

23 Ibid.

24 Ibid., 159

25 Josephus, Antiquities 15.10.3

26 The Gospels of Matthew, Mark, and Luke are referred to as the Synoptic Gospels because they include many of the same stories, often in a similar sequence and in similar or sometimes identical wording.

27 William Barclay, *The Gospel of Matthew*, [Philadelphia: Westminster Press, 1975], 2:145-146

28 The Byzantine Empire existed from 330 AD to 1453 AD.

29 Source: Website - Exploring Bible Lands, *Mount Hermon and Caesarea Philippi*, 12 July 2012

30 Matthew 16:28 - Truly, I say to you, there are some standing here who will not taste death until they see the Son of Man coming in his kingdom.

31 David McClister, From Expository Files 4.11; November 1997

32 NIV, Archaeological Study Bible, eBook: *An Illustrated Walk Through Biblical History and Culture*, Zondervan, 2010

33 Source: Website - Christ in Prophecy Journal: Explorations in Antiquity, Center - Seating At The Last Supper, December 12, 2012

34 Source: Website - Bible.org, Robert L. Deffinbaugh, *Perspective, Personal Ambition, and Prophecy* (Luke 22:24-38)

35 Luke 22:14 - And when the hour came, he reclined at table, and the apostles with him.

36 Source: Website - Christ in Prophecy Journal: Explorations in Antiquity, Center - Seating At The Last Supper, December 12, 2012

37 The Merriam-Webster Online Dictionary says a sop is "a piece of food dipped or steeped in a liquid." Sharing food with someone carried an implication of friendship and peace in the ancient world.

38 Michael Card, *A Better Freedom: Finding Life as Slaves for Christ*, 2010, p.126

39 *The Complete Works of C. H. Spurgeon*, Volume 16: Sermons 788 to 847

40 Source: Website - John Guzik, *Enduring Word*, John 13

41 Michael Card, *A Better Freedom*, p.125

42 Peter is only identified in the Gospel of John. The other gospels are silent about the person who cut off

the servant's ear. This was probably to protect the identity of Peter. John was written much later and so it was probably thought to be safe to reveal Peter's name.

43 Also known as the Sea of Galilee.

44 By 'spiritual milk' Peter means taking in God's word, and drawing close to Christ.

45 In Galatians 2:10-13, Paul challenged Peter about playing favorites between the Jews and Gentiles.

46 The sinner's prayer is a prayer a person prays to God when they understand that they are a sinner and in need of a Savior. Saying a sinner's prayer will not accomplish anything on its own.